Don-David Lusterman, Ph.D.

Infidelity

A SURVIVAL GUIDE

MJF BOOKS
NEW YORK

Published by MJF Books
Fine Communications
Two Lincoln Square
60 West 66th Street
New York, NY 10023

Infidelity: A Surival Guide
Library of Congress Catalog Card #98-74093
ISBN 1-56731-333-7

Copyright © 1998 by Don-David Lusterman

Edited by Carole Honeychurch
Text design by Tracy Marie Powell

This edition published by arrangement with New Harbinger Publications, Inc.

Manufactured in the United States of America on acid-free paper

MJF Books and the MJF colophon are trademarks of Fine Creative Media, Inc.

10   9   8   7   6   5   4   3   2   1

Contents

Acknowledgments

At the conclusion of a presentation I had just given on the subject of infidelity for a professional group, I was approached by Patrick Fanning and Matthew McKay, who told me that they'd read my professional articles on infidelity and would like me to write a book for the general public. I thank them as well as my dear friend and colleague Richard Mikesell for their initial encouragement and enthusiasm. Kristin Beck is an editor of infinite patience and equal ability. Farrin Jacobs, my interim editor, was equally helpful and encouraging. Of course, my heartfelt thanks to my final editor, Carole Honeychurch, whose skill and good humor proved invaluable. Finally, I would like to thank Tracy Marie Powell for her elegant text design.

On the home front, I must acknowledge the enormous contribution made by my wife, Judy, who has always served as my first editor, and who taught me how to tell my stories succinctly and pointedly. Finally, my thanks to my office manager and daughter-in-law Stacey, who has handled the myriad organizational tasks that accompany such an undertaking with unfailing good humor.

Introduction

Many lives are touched by infidelity. You may be reading this book because:

- you have discovered that your mate is involved in an infidelity

- you are being unfaithful and are feeling conflicted about it

- you are the "third party" in an affair and feeling uncomfortable about it

- you are the child of someone involved in an infidelity

- you are the parent of someone involved in or affected by an affair or other type of infidelity

- you are a friend, physician, psychotherapist, lawyer, or clergyperson who is helping someone troubled by an affair or other type of infidelity

Although anyone touched by infidelity can gain understanding by reading this book, it is primarily intended for married couples or couples involved in long-term, monogamous unmarried relationships. It is my hope that the book will help you to understand how infidelity comes about, what can be learned from it, and how it can be survived. People often find that once infidelity is discovered and its aftereffects are behind them, their relationship is stronger than before, and a subsequent infidelity is unlikely. For some marriages, however, infidelity is a prelude to divorce. In one particular type of infidelity, the affair, understanding what it was about and how it was rooted in the relationship can enable a couple to split (if they must) with the smallest degree of anger and acrimony. This offers any children they may have the best hope for a healthy adjustment afterward. Unmarried couples, whether they are heterosexual, gay, or lesbian, also suffer the pangs of discovered infidelity. Their feelings of betrayal are little different from those of married couples, and their process of recovery is very similar.

In order to benefit most from this book, I would urge you to keep a journal as you read. You may use it for the suggested exercises, or to note things that you have read that trigger new and helpful ideas for you. Many people find that journaling gives them some sense of power at a time in their lives when they otherwise feel that things are very out of control.

I must emphasize that not everyone is capable of recovering from infidelity solely through the assistance that reading may provide. Should you require professional help, chapter 11 will provide you with good guidelines to help you choose an appropriate person. If you do enter therapy, you and the therapist will find that your reading and journaling will help you to focus on the most important issues confronting you.

Over the years, I have spent many thousands of hours helping people with this trying problem. More recently, I've been an avid browser of the Internet, looking for bulletin boards devoted to issues connected with infidelity and corresponding with some of the bulletin board participants. I consider the understanding that I've developed to be a result of my collaboration with my patients and with my Internet correspondents, and I'd like to thank them all.

I have displayed in my waiting room a bit of Chinese calligraphy. Beneath it is written: "This is the Chinese symbol for the word 'crisis.' It consists of two words, one signifying 'danger,' the other, 'opportunity.' Are you seeing your crisis as a danger or as an opportunity?"

It is my hope that this book will help you to see, in the crisis of infidelity, the opportunity for growth and change.

Don-David Lusterman, Ph.D.

1

The Shock

of Discovery

Defining Infidelity

The word *infidelity* means the breaking of trust. When people marry they pledge before their friends, families, the state, and in most cases, their god, that they will remain faithful to one another until separated by death. Indeed, this expectation of mutual trust is the foundation of their commitment to each other. One significant element of this trust is the unspoken vow that the couple will remain sexually exclusive. Another is that there is a certain level of emotional intimacy that is reserved for the couple, not to be shared with others. Having pledged faithfulness, it is not surprising that the discoverer experiences such shock upon finding that a mate has violated it. *Infidelity occurs when one partner in a relationship continues to believe that the agreement to be faithful is still in force, while the other partner is secretly violating it.*

You do not have to be married to experience infidelity. Many people in long-term, exclusive relationships. They may remain unmarried, but in some way "wedded." This may be by mutual choice, because one partner refuses to marry, or by necessity (as is often the case with long-term gay or lesbian relationships).

Although many of the ideas and studies I've drawn upon have been derived from the study of conventional marriage, unmarried couples in long-term relationships often face the same issues. For this reason, I will sometimes refer specifically to marital issues, and at others to problems affecting all exclusive relationships.

The word "exclusive" reminds us that when we are in an intimate relationship, there are feelings and experiences that are ours alone. It's as if there is a little fence around the relationship and a sign out front that says: "Keep out—private property."

The Moment of Discovery

The moment you realize that your mate has been unfaithful you feel overwhelmed. You are flooded with thoughts: "How long has this been going on?" "Does this mean my relationship is over?" "How many other people know?" "How could I have ever trusted him?" "How could she have ever done such a thing to me?" "How could I ever trust this person again—even if I wanted to?" "Is this the first time it has happened?" "Should I confront him about this right now?" "Should I just ignore it? Maybe it's just a passing thing." "Should I set a trap?" "Should I talk with other people about it? My friend recently went through something like this—maybe it would be a good idea to talk to her about it."

Accompanying these thoughts is a rush of feelings: rage, shame, hurt, jealousy, betrayal, fear, uncertainty. Some people are so overcome at the moment of discovery that they have profound physical reactions. Many of my patients have reported bouts of vomiting or diarrhea. Others, normally the calmest of people, have screamed themselves hoarse, broken objects, or physically attacked the unfaithful mate. Some have considered suicide, others homicide.

Most of my patients report that at the moment of discovery their predominant feeling is that all hope is lost and that the relationship is over. In fact, the majority of marriages that I've treated because of infidelity have not only survived, but improved. As you read this book, you will discover that in many instances there are factors that have led to the infidelity, and that if both partners work together to repair these circumstances, their relationship will be greatly enhanced.

Just as the discoverer of infidelity suffers, the mate whose unfaithfulness is discovered may also be filled with painful thoughts and feelings. Unfaithful mates are often not at all sure that they really want to end their relationships. They seem to have put all of their thoughts and feelings about their unfaithfulness in another part of their mind, as if being unfaithful had nothing to do with their long-term relationship. Until their actions are discovered, or they sense that they are on the verge of being revealed, many people never even imagined that they would be found out.

Nor have they imagined the devastating effects on their mates, their children, their families, themselves, or the third parties. The mate who has been discovered may experience feelings and thoughts as intense as those experienced by the discoverer. One patient, Roger, told me, "I am really afraid of destroying my marriage. I can't imagine what it might do to my kids, and I'm not even sure that I really don't love my wife anymore. But I am just as fearful about losing what I've found with Sally [the other woman]. I feel so alive with her—there's so much excitement. I haven't felt like this in years." Roger also told me that he was really worried that Sally might try to retaliate in some way if he tried to cut off the relationship. Roger's fears and confusions are similar to those experienced by many people at or close to the moment of discovery.

Denial

Even though the revelation of an infidelity is overwhelming and shocking to both the discoverer and the discovered, reflection often leads them to recognize a series of actions, hints, and behaviors that preceded not only the discovery, but the infidelity itself. Each partner has been engaged in hiding many other thoughts and feelings from him- or herself, often for a long period of time.

The term describing the ability to hide things from yourself is *denial*. Denial is an unconscious act. You don't will yourself to deny—it simply happens. It can be defined as a way of resolving emotional conflict and allaying anxiety by the unconscious disavowal of thoughts that would be otherwise unbearable. In most cases, the discoverer has been increasingly plagued with fleeting thoughts that "something is wrong." Somehow these thoughts are so unacceptable that they remain in denial until the weight of evidence is so overwhelming that it must be faced. If you have recently discovered your partner's infidelity, you may now recall a series of circumstances which, with hindsight, indicated that something was going wrong. These might include changes in work habits, sudden and unexplained expenses, and even warnings from friends that they suspected something. At a deeper level, you may have been denying that there was some meaningful decline in the quality of the marriage, one that you may have ignored for a long time and never talked about. In the Introduction, I mentioned the value of keeping a journal to jot down your thoughts and feelings. Use it now to try to figure out what signals you might have been missing before that may help you to understand what was going wrong. The couple mentioned earlier, Roger and his wife Ann, began keeping journals at my suggestion after his affair came to light. Here are some entries:

Ann: For years now, almost all we ever talked about was the kids. Now I remember that whenever he wanted to do something alone with me, the kids were always with us. It's like they were a shield between us. I think he must have felt I was pushing him away. But there was stuff I was ignoring about him, stuff that should have told me something was wrong. All of a sudden his hours were changing, I couldn't get hold of him if I needed to talk to him. He didn't really seem to approach me to make love anymore. I guess because he would do it with me if I approached him, it fooled me into thinking things were okay—but it was really never that way before. He even shaved off his mustache—maybe that should have told me that he was doing it for someone else.

Roger: So many times I wanted to sit Ann down and tell her how boring things were getting between us. Maybe it wasn't true, but when I would come home from work, I felt like she couldn't have cared less. Maybe I should have said something then. I think I just buried all those thoughts. I don't know how to tell Ann when I'm angry. It always seems to make her cry—so I'm gun-shy. Maybe that's why it looked so good with Sally for a while—because I didn't have to explain anything, and I had her attention whenever I wanted it.

Sometimes There Is No Answer

Sometimes an unfaithful mate is such a skilled liar that it is all but unthinkable that an infidelity has occurred. In this situation, the many clues that are ignored when you're in denial can't be discovered, even with the virtue of hindsight. For example, Randi came to me following a discovery that was so shocking to her that she had been hospitalized with what she thought was a heart attack, which turned out to be a severe anxiety reaction. She had been in what she regarded as a "perfect" relationship. Her fiancé was very understanding, extremely thoughtful, affectionate, and considerate. Randi's folks thought that he was a perfect mate for her, and after two years of courtship, she and John had set a wedding date. Announcements were sent out, a hall was rented, and bridesmaids were chosen. A day or two before the wedding, Randi needed to check some details with him, so she decided to drop in at his apartment. She came in to find him in bed with another woman. In the months of therapy that followed, she found it impossible to find any clues that would have predicted his behavior—he had been unfailingly kind and considerate, and they had never had any sort of blowup.

Randi's distrust was so powerful that it was two years before she dared even to say hello to a man. She felt totally unprotected from future betrayal. There was absolutely nothing that she could learn from this experience that would make her a better judge of men. In one session, she told me that she wished that she *had* been in denial, because then she would have felt more prepared to be alert about possible dishonesty in her next relationship. She wasn't wrong. When you understand what you have denied, you can correct it—if not in your current relationship, at least in the next one.

Compartmentalization

When people are in denial, their unconscious plays a trick on them. It is as if all tracks of the offending thought or feeling have been obliterated. By contrast, there are situations in which people are very conscious of what they are doing, but develop the ability to disconnect that awareness from other aspects of their lives. Patrick's case is a useful example.

Patrick had been married for about ten years. At first he felt he had a perfect marriage. Over time, almost without his awareness, the joy seemed to go out of his and Charlene's relationship. As the children came along, Charlene sensed a sadness that never seemed to leave Patrick. From time to time she would try to confront him. "Is there anything wrong?" she would ask. Or, "I don't know what's the matter with you, Patrick—you used to smile all the time. I think it's been years since I saw a real smile come from deep inside of you." Try as he might, he could never name anything that would account for his sad mood. If anything, her questions simply annoyed him. Patrick wasn't lying. He was numb to his feelings. If he was occasionally aware of some feeling, such as anger at the loss of Charlene's companionship that seemed to come along with motherhood, he would dismiss it, thinking, "I guess this is just normal."

Patrick just didn't see any connection between his sadness and these thoughts. If someone had asked him at this point in his life if his marriage was all right, he would probably have said that it was—maybe not great, but certainly all right. When he drifted into an affair at work, he was mildly surprised. It seemed so out of character for him. He was very excited about the affair, because it provided him with the attention and emotional involvement that he had lost with Charlene. But if someone had asked him he would probably have said, "I just don't see the connection."

Patrick was surprised about something else as well—the energy his affair produced. He could go to work, spend hours slipping notes to his new friend, Connie, and eagerly awaiting her replies. He couldn't get her out of his mind during the work day. Sometimes they would steal away for a couple of hours to go to a motel and make love. He was amazed at how alive he felt—almost like when he had first met Charlene. The strange thing was that when he came home, Connie was all but forgotten. He could make love to Charlene, feeling no guilt or strangeness. It was as if there was one box in his mind for Charlene and another for Connie. The two boxes seemed sealed, each absolutely separate from the other. Some psychologists call this phenomenon *compartmentalization*. Unlike denial, compartmentalization is a conscious act. Patrick knew that he was having an affair. He knew he was married. He was aware that he was experiencing pleasure in the affair.

Compartmentalization and denial often exist side by side. Beyond the ability to compartmentalize the affair, the mate who has been unfaithful is often also in denial about problems in the marriage. As we have seen, Patrick was quite aware that he was excited about his affair. He remained unaware, however, of his feelings about his marriage. Because he could compartmentalize the affair, he was able to say to Charlene that he couldn't see what his office affair had to do with his marriage. Locked in separate compartments, his marriage and affair seemed to have nothing to do with each other. He believed that nothing he could do in his marriage would remove his need for the affair. Nor could he imagine himself wanting to end either his affair *or* his marriage.

Patrick's situation is not unusual. When I speak with each mate alone following the discovery of an infidelity, I often find that they have never really talked very much or very well with one another about the satisfactions and the problems that they have been experiencing in the marriage. In some types of infidelity, it is this persistent and shared denial that sets the scene for the subsequent affair. Denial and compartmentalization play different roles in various types of infidelity. We will now examine some of the ways in which infidelity occurs.

Types of Infidelity

Each type of infidelity brings with it its own problems, and each may require different types of help if the situation is to improve. As you read these descriptions, whether you are the discoverer or the discovered, try to determine which type of infidelity best describes your current situation. You may find it helpful to use your journal in comparing and contrasting your own experience to the ones described here.

One-Night Stands

Anita came to me one day in a highly agitated state. She reported to me that she had recently attended a conference out of town. There she met a man, with whom she had a few drinks and ended up in her hotel room, where they had sex. She reported that by the next morning, she was feeling awful. The night before she had felt excited and powerful, but when she awakened in the morning she felt entirely different. Her mind was racing: "Did anyone see us go off to the room? We were both drunk, and it was a stupid thing to do, as exciting as it seemed last night. What if I got a disease? Should I tell my husband?" She reported that this was the first time that it had happened, and that it was going to be the last. She said, "It's funny—it's like the time I used LSD in college. When I did it, it was kind of exciting and novel. But the next day, it really scared me that I had done it—God knows what could have happened. And because of that feeling, I never tried it again. The difference is, with the LSD I only risked hurting myself. With this thing, I risked hurting my husband and my marriage." Further conversation revealed that she felt her marriage was satisfying for both her and her husband, that their love life was excellent, and they felt, for the most part, very close and could talk easily with one another. Nonetheless, she feared his reaction should she reveal her one-night stand to him.

Philandering

I have never treated a philanderer who came willingly to therapy. Frank was no exception. He said that the only reason he had agreed to come was because his wife Jane had told him that her next move would be to see a divorce lawyer. During the first meeting, Jane could barely contain her rage. She frequently arose from her seat to pace around the room. "You've been playing around for years," she screamed. "You're all wrong," he replied. Suddenly she reached into her bag and flung a set of papers at him. "Here's your little black book," she said. I caught one of the pages. It was a computer printout containing the names of women, the towns in which he'd met them, the hotels in which they'd stayed, and what looked like some kind of rating system. Once he was confronted with this evidence, Frank admitted that Jane was right. He liked to "find, bed, and forget" a woman almost every night he was on the road. He protested (rather meekly) that he truly loved Jane, wanted desperately to continue his marriage, loved his children dearly, and didn't have the vaguest understanding of his compulsion to have these liaisons. He claimed that his love life with Jane was "just fine," and that, for the most part, his conquests brought him little sexual satisfaction. Although he was terribly frightened by Jane's anger and appeared anxious to continue the marriage, he nonetheless maintained that he couldn't understand why it was so important to her since it had no meaning to him, and always occurred "out of her sight." For him, any regret or sorrow he felt was connected only to her discovery, rather than to his actions. Had she not found out, he would have continued his customary behavior untroubled.

Affairs

When I first met Artie and Sarah, they had been married for over twenty years. They came to therapy together. Neither complained of any particular crisis that brought them to my office, but both agreed that they wanted "better communication." They did not seem very strongly motivated to make much change in what they agreed was "an okay, but not a great marriage," as Sarah described it. After a few meetings, and with no particular warning, they stopped therapy. About three years later, I received a desperate call from Artie. He had just discovered that, during the time they had been in treatment, and for several months before, Sarah had been having an affair with a mutual friend, Rich. Worst of all, the affair was on again and was now more open.

When I saw them together, Sarah for the first time admitted that she was in a relationship with Rich and that she felt very confused. She was not sure she wanted to end her marriage. Artie was a good human being, and they had shared many happy experiences. Their son was about to marry, and this seemed a particularly ironic time even to be thinking about ending their twenty-three year marriage. Yet at the same time, she could not bear the thought of giving up her relationship with Rich.

Artie was equally torn. He felt that he loved Sarah, but was enraged by her relationship with Rich. He felt bewildered and betrayed. How could he not have known? It was the lies that hurt him, even more than the realization that she had been having sex with another man. It had made their whole life together a sham. What had been true and what a lie?

Trauma

One of the common threads running through each of the three types of infidelity outlined above is the experience of trauma by each of the participants. *Trauma* may be defined as an injury caused by an external event. It derives from the Greek word meaning a wound. It is also related to the word "throe," as in "to be in the throes of a painful struggle." When people feel emotionally traumatized, this is exactly what they report. In the book *Shattered Assumptions* the psychologist Ronnie Janoff-Bulman (1992) described the effects of trauma. She reports that people who experience severe psychological trauma suffer from a shattering of their basic assumptions about the nature of the world. Before the traumatic experience, according to Dr. Janoff-Bulman, such people held three fundamental assumptions:

- The world is benevolent
- The world is meaningful
- The self is worthy

After the trauma, all three of these assumptions are called into question. Many say that their world has fallen apart. The world stinks, nothing seems to make any sense, and the sense that you know who you are and feel reasonably good about yourself is replaced by the feeling that there most be something terribly wrong with you if something so awful has happened to you. People who react to trauma this way are said to be suffering a *post-traumatic stress reaction.*

This loss of a sense of benevolence, meaning and self-worth is easily understood if we take into account most people's assumptions about marriage. Dr. Florence Kaslow (1992) studied a group of people who believed that they had good marriages. She found that the qualities most valued by these couples were "trust in each other that includes fidelity, integrity and feeling safe," and "permanent commitment to the marriage." It is reasonable to believe that most couples expect these same qualities when they marry. People who are not married also may decide to enter a monogamous relationship. For example, most people assume (even if they do not directly discuss it) that if they are engaged to be married, they will be monogamous. Even people involved in unmarried romantic relationships often hold this unspoken assumption of monogamy. High school students who are "going steady" generally expect that their relationship is exclusive and experience secret involvements with others as cheating. People who are living together, whether in heterosexual, gay, or lesbian relationships, also often agree that they are in an exclusive relationship. Cheating in these relationships is also experienced as very traumatic.

Because these assumptions are so deeply rooted in most people's ideals about romantic relationships, it should come as no surprise that their sense of the world's benevolence is severely shaken when infidelity is discovered. If you cannot believe that your own relationship is safe, how can you trust that your job will be safe, your friends will not betray you, and that everything you have trusted and believed in might not prove equally untrustworthy? The meaningfulness of your very life is called into question. People in such a situation often find themselves thinking: "What good did it do me that I was a considerate mate? That I cared for my husband when he was sick? That I comforted my wife when she lost her job? That I tolerated my intolerable in-laws in order to make things easier for my mate?" Finally, many people ask themselves, "What worth did I really have if I could be cast off with such ease?"

Not everyone who has discovered marital unfaithfulness is equally wounded, nor is every person whose infidelity is discovered equally affected. However, if you are reading this book, chances are that you, your mate, or someone with whom you are close has experienced the discovery as very traumatic. We do not know all of the reasons that make this event so much more traumatic for some people, while others seem to recover quickly. What we do know is that many people seem to find, at least at first, little strength to ward off this trauma. In fact, their every waking moment seems to be absorbed in pondering this wound and even their sleep is often severely disturbed. Mary-Jane's reaction to Carl's infidelity can help illuminate the nature of the post-traumatic reaction.

Mary-Jane was forty-six years old when I first met her. She had divorced many years ago, and it wasn't long after that she had met Carl, who had never married. Mary-Jane had a daughter, by then three years old. After the divorce, neither Mary-Jane nor her daughter had ever seen the father again. Carl not only loved Mary-Jane, but her daughter Marni as well. He lavished gifts on the little girl, helped care for her when she was ill, and acted in every way as if he was her father. Carl was the product of a divorced home, and told Mary-Jane early on that, given her angry divorce and his own parents' terrible experience, they would do better to live as man and wife but not go through a legal marriage. He even went so far as to sign over his life insurance benefits to Marni. When Mary-Jane discovered that Carl was involved with another woman, she was devastated. Carl was frightened by the intensity of her reaction. He told her that he almost immediately realized how wrong he had been and swore he would end the relationship.

Although they continued living together, she told him that she felt as if she was "living with the enemy." She said that the thought of lying in the same bed with him disgusted her. Almost anything could send her into a bout of rage or tears. Seeing a movie about unfaithfulness could result in days of rage. Hearing about a friend who discovered an infidelity could bring her to endless tears. She told him that, on some level, she knew that he was now telling the truth, but she was still plagued with dreams in which she saw him with the other woman. She relived many times over the moment that she learned of the infidelity. She could still feel the almost electric shock she experienced. She played over the events that preceded the discovery. She would try to get it off her mind, but every attempt to push it away seemed futile—if anything, it came back stronger than ever. One moment she felt that she wanted to end the relationship forever. The next, she couldn't imagine a life without him.

If your experience is similar to Mary-Jane's, and you have two or more of the following symptoms, you are probably in a post-traumatic reaction:

- difficulty falling or staying asleep
- irritability or outbursts of anger
- difficulty concentrating
- excessive vigilance—always feeling on guard
- jumping at the slightest sound
- physical reactions to reminders of the infidelity, such as nausea or shakiness

These symptoms are the usual results of the discovery of infidelity. They are not signs of mental disorder, although if they persist, it is important to see a qualified mental health practitioner in order to obtain some relief. If you are experiencing some of these symptoms now, note them in your journal. For each symptom that you have, assign a rating between one and ten. The lowest rating means that the symptom is absent. As you read on, go back to this journal entry periodically, rating the symptoms again. This will help you to see whether you are getting beyond the traumatic reaction on your own. If not, you may need the help of a mental health practitioner. In chapter 10, I will describe in more detail what sort of help is most likely to be successful and what type may be harmful.

Is the Relationship Over?

There is no simple answer to this question. Without a doubt, the discovery of marital infidelity is a crisis for all concerned. As with any crisis, there is an element of danger but also an element of hope. The first thing I tell my patients is that the outcome of this event should ideally be *change* for all concerned. I explain to them that change means that they will be moving toward a better marriage, or in some instances, a better divorce.

After thousands of hours of work with people struggling through infidelity, I have found that many couples have the capacity to emerge from this experience with new insight and new hope. However, it is very important to be aware that during the time the discoverer is experiencing a post-traumatic reaction, she or he is also probably feeling both depressed and agitated.

When you are feeling depressed, you are likely to see only the dark side of things. It is very important to remember that most people do not know with certainty what the future really holds when an infidelity is discovered. A depressed person is likely to find it hard to imagine any good coming out of this crisis. This can paralyze you, and make it impossible to take any kind of positive steps. People who are positive that their marriages are over are often proved wrong. As they mastered their depressed feelings, they felt more mobilized to take actions that have helped to correct their situation. To help counteract this understandable depression, it is important to remind yourself that the more closed off every path seems to you, the more immobilized you are likely to become. Remember, since there are often issues in the marriage that helped to trigger the infidelity, it is a real possibility that it will now be possible, working together, to correct these problems.

Agitation can also take a considerable toll. People who are agitated do not think clearly and often take very rash and impulsive actions. When the infidelity is first discovered, many people almost immediately begin to blame either their mate, the other party, or themselves. They may feel that someone must be punished, whether one of the other parties or themselves. As long as these rage-filled thoughts predominate, it's all but impossible for the couple even to begin to talk about what has gone wrong and to think about whether it can be made right or made even better than before.

In the next chapter, we will begin to examine actions that can help both the discoverer and the person who has been discovered to begin to relieve some of the pain and fear that each is suffering.

Remember

- Shock is a *normal* reaction to discovery

- The discovered person often feels as scared and confused as the discoverer

- It is unwise to take an immediate action following discovery—it's a time to reflect and reconsider

- As the dust of discovery clears, people often find that their relationship is better than before

Why Did
It Happen?

Perhaps one of the first questions that the discoverer of infidelity asks is, "Why did it happen?" There is no simple answer. Some people are unfaithful for reasons that lie deep in their past, such as a history of infidelity in their parents' marriage. Others are unfaithful because of what they believe about the opposite gender. Men who believe that women are prey to be caught, and women who believe that they are nothing without a man are caught in a way of thinking about the other gender that often leads to unfaithful behavior. For others, infidelity is rooted in the marriage itself. It is important to try to understand why an act of unfaithfulness has occurred, because once you have some sense of why it happened you can begin to consider what to do about it. This is as important for the person who is acting unfaithfully as for the one who has discovered the infidelity and just as important for the third party. One way to try to understand what causes infidelity is by describing various types of extramarital involvement.

Not All Involvements Are the Same

An *affair* takes place over time. It may be very emotionally intense, and it may or may not involve sexual intercourse. In contrast, a sexual involvement with a third party may be part of an emotional attachment, but it may also be free of it, taking little more time than the sexual act itself. People may have an affair without sex, and they may have sex without having the emotional involvement of an affair. *Once a committed relationship is established, if there is a secret sexual and/or romantic involvement outside of the relationship, it is experienced as an infidelity.*

Psychologist Fred Humphrey (1987) has spent many years studying infidelity and extramarital sex. He suggests that we can best understand any particular act by considering the many factors involved. For one thing, you may want to know how long an extramarital affair has been going on. If your partner has been involved with more than one person, how often has it happened and with how many partners? It may also help to know whether there was a strong emotional bond between your mate and the other person. Some people find it very important to know whether there was sexual intercourse; others are much more upset about a strong emotional attachment.

For many people, the secrecy involved in extramarital activities is the most hurtful thing. For others, the discovery that one's mate is secretly involved in a gay or lesbian relationship is especially confusing and painful. Understanding the elements of any particular act of infidelity can shed light on why it happened. The more emotional we feel about something, the less clearly we can think about it. Standing back, examining what has happened, and opening dialogue about it can help an individual or a couple get beyond the initial shock of discovery.

Using this logic, let's examine some examples of extramarital involvements. Dan, for example, had frequent one-night stands with no emotional involvement. Another patient, Laura, was involved in a lengthy emotional but nonsexual affair. These two situations are very different, although each is a type of infidelity. Dan's frequent and secret escapades with many partners may have no emotional meaning for him, but they certainly put him at particular risk for sexually transmitted diseases. While Dan's wife might feel relieved to hear that his extramarital activities were neither emotional nor long-standing, she might well be frightened of contracting a disease from him. She might also feel hurt and angry because of all his lying to cover his adventures. Laura's husband is confronted with a wife who is involved in a long-term relationship with one man. He may need to talk with her not only about his hurt, but also about what emotional needs are being fulfilled in her affair that are not being met in their marriage. He may see her affair as the inevitable end of the marriage. Laura, however, may feel that telling her husband offers one last chance to see how much change the marriage will need in order to be successful for her. Maybe, she thinks, this will finally make him see how much she wants a deeper emotional involvement from him.

Are Men's and Women's Extramarital Involvements Different?

It isn't surprising that Laura is looking for greater emotional involvement, while Dan seems to be looking for a variety of sexual experiences. Men and women often seek different things when they become involved in extramarital activity. Research by two psychologists, Shirley Glass and Thomas Wright (1995), shows that there are important differences that determine why men and women become involved extramaritally. Glass and Wright found that women are more likely to link sex with love, while men's involvements are more often primarily sexual.

This is, of course, not true of all men or all women. Some men view an affair as a return to romance and excitement and an escape from day-to-day responsibilities. Some women feel that extramarital sex, with no emotional entanglement, adds spice to their lives. In many instances, the beliefs that people hold about why people stray make it difficult for a couple to communicate when an infidelity is discovered. For example, Dan's wife may find it hard to accept his explanation that he was simply sexually curious, that his many involvements with other women had nothing to do with love, and certainly were not intended to hurt her. In her mind, sex and emotional commitment are locked so tightly together that she can't imagine one without the other. Similarly, Laura's husband would probably accuse her of lying if she said that she had never had intercourse but craved only the emotional attention and kindness that she had experienced in her affair. He believes that if a man gets close to a woman, he has only one goal in mind—to have sex with her.

So we can see how the beliefs that men and women hold about each other's extramarital activities can get in the way of honest communication. For this reason, it isn't surprising to hear a man who strays claim that his marriage is good—and really mean it. Such a man may see his exploits as a male privilege that has nothing whatever to do with his feelings about his marriage. Women who stray are much more likely to feel great disappointment in the emotional side of their marriage and finally reach a point where they look beyond their marriage for emotional comfort; of course, men too may have an affair because of marital disappointment.

In our attempt to understand why extramarital behavior occurs, let's begin with some of the most frequent reasons given for various types of infidelity. If some of these items ring true for you, use your journal to examine them. If there is an issue that you think is important to your situation that is not on this list, be sure to include it in your own journal entry.

- Not understanding what relational love is

- Inability to communicate feelings or needs

- Not having the verbal skills to solve problems together

- Not being able to accommodate to one another's needs or interests

- Not really knowing the person you married (for example—unaware of some upsetting sexual problem)

- Not being able to cope with cultural or ethnic differences

- Unrealistic expectations about the nature of marriage

- Disappointment that your mate has not grown in the same ways you have

- Sexual curiosity

- Emotional need (feeling lonely in the relationship and looking elsewhere)

- Sexual addiction

- Boredom

- Losing the sense of fun and excitement you once had as a couple

- Getting so caught up in life's daily obligations that you lose sight of one another

As you continue reading, compare your journal entry to the specific explanations that various authorities have proposed, which I've outlined below. You will see later that understanding why an infidelity occurs has many benefits. It will help to determine what the chances are that the relationship will survive the infidelity, what approach the discoverer should take, how the involved partner can resolve his or her own feelings about staying in the marriage, and what kind of treatment would be most helpful. As you read ahead, look for any issue that you think is relevant to your own situation.

The Life Crisis Theory

There is a series of events that most people have either already experienced or will experience in their life time. These include: meeting who you think of as the "ideal person" to spend your life with; mutually deciding to marry or enter a long-term, exclusive relationship; having a child; getting a promotion at work; buying a first house. Many people think of these events as milestones in their lives—events that mark increasing maturity and responsibility. You may also experience other, more painful milestones as you pass through life. These might include: losing a child; feeling rejected by a mate; losing a parent; losing a job.

Each of the above events, whether positive or negative, produces a certain amount of stress. Think first of the negative events. It isn't hard to understand the pain of loss, whether it's losing a parent, a child, or a job. But positive events also can produce stress. One might feel: "Have I really chosen the right mate?" "Am I truly ready for the responsibilities of parenthood?" "Can I really fulfill people's expectations as I undertake this new job?" "Now that our children are grown, what is left of my marriage?"

Thus you can see that either positive or negative life changes can cause stress and anxiety. If both members of a couple are good at talking about these stresses, they usually weather them together, and their relationship becomes even deeper and more satisfying. For example, when Ned received an important promotion he told Beverly, "I know I'm excited about this, but I'm also kind of scared. I hope I've really got the ability to succeed at this. And what if I mess it up? Will I be out of a job?" Beverly listened, accepted his fears, and even shared some of her own concerns. Such a couple is developing a way to get through the first tough weeks of the new job because they can speak openly about it. More than that, because they are talking with each other about an important event in their lives, they are growing closer together. The ability to trust one another enough to talk honestly about what you are feeling, even if it is negative—to reveal yourself safely, to openly express needs, disappointments, longings and pleasure—are all aspects of intimacy.

Another man, filled with the same excitement and the same doubts, says nothing to his wife—perhaps because he doesn't know how to or because he feels it makes him look less of a man. Jack, a thirty-five-year-old stockbroker, came to therapy because his wife discovered that he had been seeing a call girl for several months. As we talked in therapy, it came out that he began his involvement with the call girl the day of his promotion to section manager. He had always prided himself on being a "heavy hitter" financially, and he described himself as the kind of guy who never takes his troubles home. Like his father, he had learned to suppress his anxiety because talking about it might make him seem weak to his wife. He said that when he was with the call girl, he felt absolutely at ease because his every need was attended to, and he didn't have to ask her for anything. He never talked with her about the stress he was under, but he felt that simply being in this situation gave him the relief that he wanted. He also felt ashamed that he had done it and frightened that his wife might leave him over it.

Almost every therapist has encountered a young husband who had sex with someone on the very night that his wife was giving birth. One patient explained to me that he had never felt so alone, incompetent, or useless as he did leaving the hospital following his daughter's birth. He said, "It's like I had no *purpose* being there. I felt like I was just in the way. It's like, becoming a mother, she was in a different place." He went out, had a few drinks at a local bar, and ended up having drunken sex with a woman he met there. Other men feel rejected by their wives because of the intense bonding they see between their wife and baby, a bonding that seems to squeeze them out. They see their wives as tired, preoccupied, and uninterested in sex. One patient told me that this filled him with despair and led him to an affair that spanned several months. Women are similarly vulnerable after the birth of a child. Annette, a thirty-two-year-old account executive, was thrilled after the birth of her first baby. She found herself increasingly angered, however, by her feeling that her husband Al seemed so uninvolved in caring for the baby. She began to feel that the baby and the home were a second job she had to take on alone. Attempts to talk about this with Al led to angry fights that never seemed to get resolved. When she met a man at work who found her attractive and made no secret about it, it was not long before she was intensely infatuated with him. Soon after, her office romance began.

Mid-Life Crisis

A person's life, like any good story, has a beginning, a middle, and an end. It isn't surprising that many people, as they approach what they think of as the midpoint of their life, undertake a kind of review. You may find yourself thinking, "What have I accomplished, and will I continue to accomplish? Am I satisfied with the course that my life has taken? Can it get better? Am I disappointed in how my life is going? Can I change it? What would be the price of change? For myself? For my mate? For my children?" The more you think, the more questions flood your mind.

The psychologist Dan Levinson (1978) has studied the impact of developmental change on men's lives. He describes this process as "mid-life evaluation." Others call it a mid-life crisis or "male menopause." Although Levinson entitled his book "The Seasons of a Man's Life," there is reason to believe that as many women as men begin at mid-life to consider these same questions. The psychiatrist Frank Pittman (1989, 1993), an authority on marital infidelity, describes three separate mid-life crises that often trigger an act of infidelity. The first is called the "empty nest" crisis, which occurs as the last child grows up and leaves home. Now that the children are grown, the couple must consider what is left of their marriage. Is the fire out? Can it be relit?

A second mid-life crisis is what Pittman calls "reaching the summit." Men are particularly likely to experience this particular crisis, but as more women enter the competitive world of business and professional life, they also are likely to experience it. Arriving at the summit often includes the feeling that there is no place to go now but down. This often causes feelings of depression or panic in the growing realization that the dizzying pace cannot be maintained forever. Many men have been so trained to succeed that they have no idea what their lives would be like without the degree of power, money, and success that they have finally achieved.

Pittman details a third crisis, which may or may not occur at mid-life, called "the facts of life" crisis. Unlike the summit or the empty nest crises, a sudden awareness of "the facts of life" can occur earlier or later than mid-life, but like these other crises, "the facts of life" crisis is a frequent trigger for extramarital activity. "At some point in the course of the marriage," says Pittman, "people come to grips with several painful realities. They are imperfect, their spouse is imperfect, their children are imperfect, they are not going to conquer the world . . . and it will all get worse." These thoughts have enormous power. Like the empty nest and summit crises, this realization can also cause great anxiety or overwhelming depression. When people are anxious or depressed, they often set upon solutions that, at least for the moment, seem to relieve these feelings. One quick fix is to find a new love; to regain the feeling of a new future, with new possibilities.

Entitlement

The feminist movement has worked hard to increase people's awareness about men's attitudes toward women. Despite these gains, many people still believe that it is perfectly all right for men to eye women, make suggestive remarks to them, and view them as objects rather than as living people. This message is delivered in many ways. We see it in TV advertisements, in magazines, and in the movies. Many people continue to hold the belief that if a woman "gets into trouble" with a man, she somehow has brought it on herself. Men who buy the message that women are their playthings are more likely to have sexual affairs to which they attach no emotional meaning. The psychologists Glass and Wright report that 56 percent of men who had purely sexual extramarital involvements reported that their marriages were happy, as do 33 percent of women. Clearly, there is a group of people who believe that extramarital *sex*, as opposed to extramarital *romance*, has nothing to do with their marriage. Men and women who feel this way never find their way into a therapist's office until one of two things happen: they are caught by their partner, or they begin to feel that they are falling in love with someone with whom they have been having sex, and that this means that their long-term relationship or marriage is over.

There is another form of entitlement that seems to strike men and women more equally. This is the belief that marriage should meet all their needs. One such need is for constant attention, another is for consistently great sex. Another belief is that women are responsible for relationships. Those who accept this see a wife's role as keeping her husband content and satisfied. For some women this becomes a full-time occupation. Barbara told me, "I did everything I knew how to keep my husband happy. I learned from my mother that my job was to create a beautiful and serene home, to dress well (meaning the way he liked), to keep myself well groomed, and to protect him from the children's little squabbles." In return, she felt entitled to his continual shows of interest and to his large income, which had given the family many material advantages. Her husband Bob said that he had learned that his job was to be the provider. He felt that he was supposed to handle life outside the home, and that it was her responsibility to make the home a safe and welcome place for him. This was how his parents' marriage had worked, and it seemed good enough for them. Through the years, both Barbara and Bob had played their roles so well that once the children had grown, they felt they barely knew one another and were left with little to share. They came to therapy because each one of them had discovered that the other was having an affair. Both were seeking in their affairs the feelings of closeness and sharing that they had lost through the years.

Sexual Identity Affairs

Many people grow up with very conflicted feelings about their own sexual identity. For many people, the issue reaches crisis proportions during adolescence. A boy may find himself attracted to girls but also to boys. A girl may find herself cold to the advances of boys but feeling a deep crush on another girl. A boy may be plagued by thoughts of having sex with a much younger girl. Adolescents learn quickly that they must be very secretive about these thoughts because they can experience much cruelty from others if these thoughts and impulses are openly admitted. For some, the internal pressure is so strong that it must be acknowledged and dealt with. It is at this point that a person will openly declare, "I am gay," or "I am a lesbian," or "I am bisexual." For others, these thoughts remain deeply buried, coming to light only much later in life. The lessons of secrecy have been well learned. At some point in a person's life, these long-suppressed thoughts may suddenly erupt. The person is forced into exploring these old feelings.

Doug's wife Eunice told me: "The fact that Doug was having a gay relationship hit me like a ton of bricks. He is a minister and, I always thought, a good Christian. He is a good father and a great parson and preacher. Everyone loves him, and the weirdest part is, we always had a good love life—at least I thought we did. He is considerate, gentle, and interested in my pleasure." Doug explained that, as a teenager, he had feelings toward other boys, but he had done nothing about it because he thought it was sinful and wrong. He had never dated much but when he became a seminary student he began to feel that it was important to find the right woman to marry and he had never felt that he did not love and respect her. He said, "In a way, it was like being a sleepwalker. I went through the marriage always trying to be a good husband and a good man but always feeling that, in some way, I was not sure that this was *me*, at least not the real and true me." At a convention, he met a man to whom he felt deeply attracted. He had a drink or two and found himself in the man's hotel room, where for the first time in his life he had gay sex. He was filled with excitement, shame, and guilt. He said nothing to Eunice, but she noticed that he had come back from the meeting not quite himself. Neither of them is sure that this means the end of their marriage, but it's left each with many questions about Doug's sexual identity.

Adrienne's situation is quite different. She married at sixteen to escape a brutal home life where she was frequently beaten and often saw her mother suffer serious physical injuries at her father's hands. She met Mario, a twenty-eight-year old man who seemed the answer to her dreams. He always seemed to have money in his pocket, courting her with a stream of expensive gifts. A few times during their whirlwind courtship she suspected that he was playing around with other women, but he assured her that she was mistaken. A couple of times when they were at parties he became jealous. A fight erupted between them and he would hit her, but she thought, "At least it was for a reason—not like my father, who hits for nothing." They married within a few months of meeting and had, within a space of seven years, six children. During this time the fights escalated.

Adrienne gradually became aware that Mario was a compulsive gambler, and that in his gambling episodes, he frequented prostitutes. She also discovered that he was in deep trouble because of gambling debts and had already used up a considerable amount of their savings. With all this, she continued to crave his attention and love, but he seemed increasingly distant. If she pressed for attention, he would disappear for a few days, a week, and finally, for months. One day, during one of Mario's increasingly frequent absences, Adrienne met a woman at a church dinner who seemed kind and attentive, providing a sympathetic ear for stories about Mario and the marriage. The relationship between Adrienne and Florrie gradually deepened.

One day, Florrie called Adrienne and told her that she must see her immediately. She explained to Adrienne that she was a lesbian, that she felt enormously attracted to Adrienne, and could not continue the friendship if it did not include romantic love and affection. Their relationship moved rapidly from exploratory kisses and hugs to a full sexual relationship, and for the very first time in her life, Adrienne experienced orgasm. She felt so confused. Did her affair with Florrie mean that she was a lesbian, or perhaps bisexual?

When Mario discovered the affair, he immediately filed for divorce. It was at this point that Adrienne noticed that her passion for Florrie was ebbing. For the first time, she admitted to herself how many things about Florrie really bothered her, especially how Florrie, very much like Mario, wanted control of her life. Adrienne eventually came to the conclusion that her sexual relationship with Florrie was an experiment that she wished she had made in high school. She felt that what she really craved was a tender relationship with a man, something she had never known. What she learned from Florrie was that, locked within her, was a sexually alive self. A few years later, she found herself in a relationship with a man who respected her and did not control her. Now she knew that she could be safe enough with a man to permit herself to be sexually fulfilled. Speaking about her confusion with a therapist a few years later, she said, "I think my awakening could have come from any one, whether man or woman, who showed me the slightest kindness."

Sexual Addiction and Don Juanism

The term *sexual addiction* refers to a compulsive need to engage in sexual experiences. These experiences are nonrelational—they are not romanticized, as affairs usually are. The psychologists Ralph Earle and Gregory Crowe (1989) list a series of attributes that they believe all addicts share. People who are sexually addicted generally show all or most of the following characteristics:

- a tendency to hold low opinions of themselves and to constantly remind themselves of their deficiencies

- distorted or unrealistic beliefs about themselves, their behavior, other people, and the events that occur in the world around them

- a desire to escape from or to suppress unpleasant emotions

- difficulty coping with stress; at least one powerful memory of an intense high experienced at a crucial time in their lives and an ever-present desire to recapture the euphoric feeling

- an uncanny ability to deny that they have a problem

Philanderers crave quick sexual adventures. Romance doesn't interest them at all. Most Don Juans are men, although occasionally we find a woman Dona Juana. People who philander are very different from those who have affairs. In an affair there is a third person who has become an important part of the life of the involved partner. When an affair occurs, the mate can often see some relationship between the way the marriage was going and the onset of the affair. With philandering, however, the quality of the marriage is not the real issue. The problem of Don Juanism lies deep within the Don Juan, and its solution depends upon whether he (in some cases, she) is ready to face it.

Philanderers may appear to be very strong and successful people, but inside, they feel empty. Each conquest leaves them with a fleeting feeling that they are powerful, attractive, and wanted by another human being. The purpose of the philandering is to bring relief to a person who really doesn't feel at all good about him- or herself. Like any other addiction, the initial "hit," whether it is the first sniff of cocaine, the first cigarette, or the first conquest, has a powerful effect. That intensity can never be recaptured. Each subsequent experience is a little weaker in its power to produce the original feeling, but the addict feels ever more drawn to the addiction because it filled the emptiness that is so central to his life.

Don Juans feel compelled to go through the experience of finding some person to "conquer," spend as little time as possible scheming to get them into bed, and then, having accomplished this goal, leave. These sexual partners are seen not as people, but as wanted objects. They have no meaning beyond this. The next day, addicts once again begin their feverish search, although it may be days, weeks, or months before they "score" again. Being "successful," however, only lasts for a while, and they continue to be driven to try with some new person.

Don Juans report that their need to sexually conquer began some time during their adolescence. This was when they first discovered that, at least for a short period of time, the conquest added excitement to their life. Young Don Juans are not like other adolescents in at least one important way. They seldom develop a first, serious high school relationship with one particular person, but if they do, it's likely to be an emotionally distant one. A Don Juan's romantic partner will sense this unwillingness to commit emotionally, but will often have difficulty putting a finger on exactly what was wrong. Lisa and Jared provide a good example.

"He's such a nice boy," Lisa, a high-schooler, told me as she spoke of her boyfriend Jared, "but I really don't know who he is." Her attempts to dig deeper into him frustrated and angered her. She felt she loved him but she just couldn't get close. She also felt that he was extremely controlling of her. She could do almost nothing without some criticism (because he loved her so much, he said—he wanted her to be at her best). Lisa and Jared had agreed that their relationship was "exclusive." From time to time, Lisa complained of his unexplained absences. When she questioned him, he would become very evasive and defensive. Eventually he became enraged and verbally abusive. During a particularly bitter fight, the truth came out. He had been having what he called "brief flings" with a number of other girls. Lisa couldn't believe what he was telling her. It seemed so foreign to the Jared that she knew. How could this be?

The psychiatrist James Masterson (1988) describes young people like this, those who have remarkable problems with intimacy and poor impulse control, as "lacking a real self." Masterson draws on the work of the British psychoanalyst D. W. Winnicott (1965), who describes how people develop what he calls a "false self." The false self is the self that people present to the world in order to get the praise, love, and approval that they didn't receive in the early years of life. If a person could be just him- or herself growing up, and feel warmly accepted, there would be little need for a false self. It is a mask. People who are maltreated and feel unloved in early life are protected by this mask. The mask is not simply the face that they present to others. It is also their way of avoiding the painful thoughts, conflicts, and emotions that they experienced as young children.

Dr. Patrick Carnes (1983), an authority on sexual addiction, says that addicts typically engage in a number of characterstic behaviors that include using denial, distorting reality to maintain their own sense of safety, ignoring their problems, and involving themselves in impulsive, self-destructive behaviors. The addiction may involve having sex with many people, but the object for the sexually addicted person is to fill an inner void. A good example is Jason, a forty-year-old salesman, who came to my office because of his wife's fear that he was addicted to cocaine. She told him that if he didn't get some help with this, she would leave him. She felt that his habit left him irritable and unpredictable, and that it was using up a great amount of their income. However, when Jason spoke with me alone, a very different picture emerged. He told me that he had been a very shy boy and felt absolutely unable to develop a relationship with a girl while in high school. "If there had been an award for class nerd," he told me, "I would have earned it."

When he arrived at college, he felt just as socially inept. One day, a fraternity brother asked him if he had ever been with a prostitute. He and his friend soon found themselves in a house of prostitution where, for the first time in his life, Jason experienced sex with another person. He told me that it left him with very confused thoughts. One was that having sex was exciting, dirty, and secret. Another was that he would not have the courage to go back and seek it out alone, without his fraternity brother. A third was that he didn't have to worry about his lack of social skill, because, as he said, "She did it all for me."

Jason found that the secret to finding the courage to go back was to get high, first on alcohol—which he found made it hard for him to have an erection—and later marijuana, which he felt made him feel more sexually alive. To the present day drug use was invariably part of his sexual life and always occurred as he was seeking prostitutes or when he was with them. He also said that he was becoming panicked about his problem, because now he found himself craving the experience several times a week. He also told me that he loved his wife very much, and so it was very important to him that his wife never discover his sexual addiction. He was more than happy to "take the rap" for a drug addiction, even to go to a treatment center for it, but, as he said, "It won't help, because that's not the real problem."

Don Juans are very similar to sexually addicted people, with one major difference. They tend to hold high opinions of themselves, and are, for the most part, blissfully unaware of their deficiencies. While a sexually addicted person often feels a great deal of shame and guilt (as did Jason), many Don Juans feel comfortable with their own behavior. In chapter 1, we examined the case of Frank and Jane. Frank, you will remember, kept a "little black book" in which he listed his many sexual conquests. He claimed that he felt the need to "find, bed, and forget" a woman almost every night he was on the road as a salesman. Like Jason, Frank claimed that he loved his wife and wanted to continue his marriage. But unlike Jason, Frank showed no guilt or shame about his behavior. It was impossible at first for Frank to understand why Jane was so upset about discovering his "little black book." It was only her discovery that upset him, not his own actions, which, as he said, were his "private business."

Exploratory Affairs

Unlike the "accidental" affairs that we talked about earlier, exploratory affairs have a more deliberate quality. An exploratory affair is more likely to occur when a person becomes deeply aware that a marriage is in trouble but has not yet clearly resolved whether to stay or to leave. Cheryl, for example, had spent years trying to "reform" Cliff. All he seemed to want to do was work, come home, open a bottle of beer, sit on the couch, and watch whatever sports event happened to be on. He was angry with her if the house was not in perfect order and, if the children bothered him while he was watching the TV, he would become so enraged that it scared her. Their love life had come to a grinding halt. "There was a time when he was my friend, and I could talk things over with him—but no more," she said. Cheryl was becoming more discouraged every day. Sitting at her computer one evening, she began to surf the Internet and found herself drawn to a chat line called "Lonely and Looking." "Something clicked in me," she reported. "It seemed like a perfect description of where I was in my life." After a few visits to a chat line, it wasn't long before she began an e-mail correspondence with a man who seemed to be sensitive, interested in her feelings, and as lonely as she.

Eventually a personal meeting was arranged, and she and the man had a brief affair. At first he seemed wonderful and caring, but it wasn't long before she realized that he was a problem drinker. She also learned that, at forty years of age, he still lived with his aging parents. Later she could see that this brief fling, and a few others that followed, gave her a chance to see what it was like "out there." She began to sense that some of the problems she had with her husband could as easily occur with other men. She decided to throw all of her energy into a new attempt to re-examine not only her husband's part in the decline of the marriage, but her own as well.

While some exploratory affairs end with the realization that the marriage can improve, others end in a decision to divorce. One man explained to me that, in his exploratory affairs he got his feet wet. When he felt sufficiently strong he was able to end his marriage and move on with his life.

Tripod Affairs

People may choose to stay in an unhappy marriage for a variety of reasons. These include fear of the economic consequences of leaving, fear of the impact on children, worry about the effect of divorce on their status in the community, and concern about its effect on aging parents. In order to maintain a marriage that is so lacking in positive feeling, some people find another person who fulfills the needs that they feel cannot be fulfilled in the marriage. It is as if the marriage couldn't stand on its own two feet, so a third party is added for support, just as the third leg of a tripod adds support. The third party may provide companionship, sexual fulfillment, tenderness, even adventure. Often the affair-involved person believes that it is the affair that holds the marriage together. In some cases this is true. I have treated marriages that have involved a third party for many years. However, in many of these cases, there is evidence that the noninvolved mate is aware of the affair, or at least strongly suspects it, but never directly challenges the mate. In this sort of relationship, the tripod affair seems more like a covert or maybe even an overt agreement by husband and wife to maintain the marriage by means of the affair.

More often however, the noninvolved mate is not conscious of the affair. As in any protracted affair, there is a chain of lies that supports the second relationship. When the affair is revealed, the noninvolved mate is hurt and enraged. This rage is not lessened by the mate's protestations that the last thing he or she wanted was to end the marriage. In many instances, if the marriage does end, the affair-involved mate almost immediately experiences pressure from the third person to marry. It is often at this point that the new relationship becomes strained. Many tripod relationships then break apart. I have often heard patients tell me, after the breakup of first their marriage, followed by the ending of their tripod affair, that they couldn't believe how blind they had been to the faults of the person with whom they were having the affair. In many instances, people later regret that they couldn't see their affair as an unheeded sign that their marriage was in trouble.

People may also choose to stay in a marriage with a chronically ill or debilitated mate, both for the reasons mentioned above and out of compassion. In such cases, there may be an open agreement, or the ill mate may be so debilitated that communication is not possible.

Retaliatory Affairs

Sometimes the offended mate responds by having an affair as an act of retaliation. It has been my experience that women are more likely to have retaliatory affairs. Perhaps this is because of differences in power between many men and women. A man's act in a similar situation might be to express his anger by leaving the marriage. A woman may feel less able to do so, either because her concept of marriage does not allow leaving it, or because she fears the consequences for herself and her children. For this reason, most retaliatory affairs are expressions of helpless rage and pow-erlessness. These affairs are particularly joyless. Their purpose is really more to hurt the offending partner than to bring joy to the retaliating person. They usually are not intended to end the mar-riage, although occasionally the mate's reaction to the retaliation is to seek a divorce. The best that can be said of retaliatory affairs is that, for some people, they seem to even the score. But they do not help the couple resolve the problems that led to either the original affair or the retaliatory affair.

Exit Affairs

You've seen that in exploratory, tripod, and retaliatory affairs, the affair-involved mate may be unsure of whether he or she wants the marriage to end. In an exit affair, the affair-involved mate has already made that decision, although his or her mate may not yet know it. Many therapists have met a couple in the throes of an exit affair. Often a man will bring his wife to therapy, hoping that the therapist can prop her up as he prepares to leave. He will come armed with a list of complaints, including her depression and irritability. It has been my experience that many people in-volved in exit affairs don't want to be seen as bad people, and so they subtly (or not so subtly) throw the blame onto their mate. As their mate's rage overflows at the moment of discovery, this offers further proof to the offending mate of how bad things have al-ways been. In addition, seeing the other person as "the problem" may also help to justify unethical behavior.

Elyssa called me to make an appointment for her husband Eric, who had become increasingly depressed over what he sus-pected was an affair that she was conducting with a recently wid-owed neighbor. Elyssa had given him countless assurances that it was "all in his head." I asked her if she would accompany him to therapy, but she insisted that he come alone. "Eric's got a lot of stuff he has to work out," she told me, "including not just how de-pressed he is, but also how jealous he can become." In therapy, he revealed how Elyssa seemed to be making herself more and more scarce around the house, how he was often left alone at night to take care of the kids, and how lame Elyssa's excuses seemed.

Eric felt that there were problems in the marriage on both sides, and that it would be good if he and Elyssa could come in and talk about them together. He believed there was an affair, but felt that it might be symptomatic of problems in the marriage, problems he was willing to talk about with her in therapy.

When Elyssa agreed to come, she at first denied the affair. After a few sessions she admitted that, yes, she was having an affair, but still wanted to talk about the marriage. In the sessions, she seemed blaming and distant. Even if Eric became teary-eyed, she didn't reach out or offer any support. When he suggested a trial separation, she was strongly opposed. A few days after that session, a very panicked Eric called to tell me that he had been served with divorce papers, and that Elyssa had used the last few months to empty some funds from their joint account. He was in a state of shock. After the papers were served, she told him that he had been right from the beginning, but that she felt absolutely driven to be with her new lover and to end the marriage. She believed that bringing him to therapy was a way of providing some emotional cushion for him as she moved toward the divorce. But it made him feel all the more betrayed and alone.

In this chapter we examined some of the factors that draw people into extramarital involvements. We noted that some of these involvements grow out of very obvious marital problems, while others seem to come out of the blue. As you read this chapter, you may have found yourself thinking that one particular scenario was exactly what happened in your marriage. More likely, you have seen aspects of several cases that seem to relate to your own situation. We have seen that there are many types of infidelity, but that only in one—the lengthy affair—is there an ever-present, although unacknowledged, third partner. Because this is such a special and complicated type of infidelity the next chapter will deal only with affairs.

Remember

- Some unfaithfulness is sexual but not emotional

- Some unfaithfulness is emotional but not sexual

- Sometimes it is easy to see where the relationship is going wrong and why that made infidelity more possible

- Sometimes the unfaithfulness has its roots in deep problems of the unfaithful partner

- Some involvements are clearly meant as a signal that the involved person wants out of the relationship

- In many cases, the involvement is a "wakeup call" for a re-examination of the relationship

The Affair
Triangle

The idea that love and marriage are intimately connected runs very deep. A popular song tells us, "Love and marriage go together like a horse and carriage—you can't have one without the other." A smile comes to our faces, because we feel intuitively that it hits the nail on the head. Love and marriage *do* go together.

But there's a dark underside to this sentiment. After all, if love and marriage go together so naturally, then no longer feeling "*in* love" must mean that your marriage is in deep trouble. Some people begin to panic as they lose this infatuated feeling. They confuse being "in love" with the more complex idea of *married* love, and become desperate to recapture that lost feeling. This often triggers the start of an affair. This chapter is not about Don Juanism or about one-night stands, because affairs have a logic of their own. To best understand that logic, we will start by examining the roles that love and infatuation play in marriage.

Love and Infatuation

Since for most people, infatuation is an aspect of "falling in love," it is easy to mistake infatuation *for* love. When you feel infatuated, you feel captivated or charmed by someone, whether it be an acquaintance, a movie star, or a lover. You're fascinated. You can't get the person out of your mind. You're obsessed. You see no flaws. Most people report that at some point in their courtship, they had similar feelings about the person they decided to marry. While not every marriage begins with feelings of infatuation, it happens so frequently that it is worth some attention.

Infatuation is often the characteristic feeling in an affair, never evolving into a more tempered, realistic, and mature love. An affair, by its very nature a secret liaison, locks the object of your infatuation with you in a private world. Since there are few, if any, opportunities to expose your perceptions of this person to the light of day, it is especially easy to maintain your illusions. You romanticize. You see the object of your desire as what you want, but not necessarily as what they are. Thus, the infatuation can continue, untested.

By contrast, when you have made a commitment to marry, you're anxious to introduce your intended to friends and family. When you do, you are often subjected to questions that challenge your most cherished ideas about the object of your love. "She's a lovely woman, but she seems so short-tempered." Or, "He certainly doesn't seem to like to part with a penny." Everyone seems to have a thought, and some of them cause even the most convinced person to think of the object of his or her ardor in a somewhat different way. So the ideas that you developed in the infatuation stage of courtship are put under the pressure of public scrutiny, helping you move from infatuation to a more balanced, reality-based love.

While many marriages begin with infatuation, some do not. Until the end of the nineteenth century, most marriages were arranged. Considerable thought was given then to those cultural and religious similarities that often help a marriage to get off on the right foot. There is little reason to believe that these marriages fared any worse than do those in our own time. Even today not all people marry for romantic reasons. The age at which people make the commitment to marry is rising. Many people make the decision to marry because they feel that time is running out. They then seek out an available person, not necessarily a "heartthrob."

Why Warts Are Important

Winston Churchill was Prime Minister of Britain during the course of the Second World War. He was a prominent statesman, but far from the most handsome of men. When he sat for a state portrait by an artist known for painting his subjects in the best possible light, he instructed him: "Paint me warts and all."

If we are lucky, the scrutiny of your family and friends helps the love that leads to marriage become deeper than the infatuation with which it may have started. It helps bring you to a more realistic understanding of your mate-to-be, "warts and all." And, it is a two-way process, which at its best enables each person to become more realistic about their partner. The mutual acceptance of each other as living people, with flaws and virtues, lays the groundwork for a realistic marriage. As their courtship progresses, people who have undergone this process feel more prepared for the ups and downs that are an invariable aspect of married life.

The psychiatrist Aaron Beck (1988) wrote a book about marriage called, appropriately enough, *Love Is Never Enough*. In it, he describes the qualities that he believes are necessary for a successful marriage:

> Special personal qualities are crucial for a happy relationship: commitment, sensitivity, generosity, consideration, loyalty, responsibility, trustworthiness. Mates need to cooperate, compromise, and follow through with joint decisions. They have to be resilient, accepting, and forgiving. They need to be tolerant of each other's flaws, mistakes and peculiarities.

These qualities are, in many ways, the very opposite of those we feel while infatuated. In our infatuation, the other person is unreal, more a product of our imagination than a real person. Everything seems perfect. There is little to negotiate. Things seem entirely rosy. But when an affair has ended, people almost invariably comment on how amazed they were that they had so misread the person with whom they were involved.

Those who are lucky in their courtship have begun to develop the ability to look at their mates-to-be realistically. For many, however, the decision to marry occurs in the flush of infatuation. As the disagreements that are part of any relationship multiply, such people are apt to feel disillusioned. Having illusions is, unfortunately, the best preparation for disillusionment. It is easy to confuse the loss of illusion with the loss of love. This can have disastrous consequences. It can lead a person to the false conclusion that the marriage is over; or it can produce a vague, unnameable restlessness. Those who lack the tools to talk about feelings then become particularly vulnerable to an affair.

Most people do not think, "It's time for an affair." They feel as if it has simply fallen into their lives. When the affair happens, it often makes the marriage seem pale by comparison. One woman, who eventually returned to her husband after a passionate affair, told me, "As I became more and more involved with my lover, every little fault in my husband became magnified. For a time, I could see not the slightest good in him. I think the fact that I felt so in love in my affair made me *need* to feel that I no longer loved my husband. Otherwise I would have felt like a very bad person, and I'm not really. So, having convinced myself that loving my boyfriend meant I no longer loved my husband, having the affair made perfect sense." Because she felt this way, she was able to feel ever more justified in continuing her affair. She also reported, "It's weird, I've always prided myself on being a wonderful mother, but during the affair, I scarcely thought about the kids. My mind was in another place. It's as if a marriage kind of has its own rhythm, and I lost the beat."

Married Love vs. Affair Love

Marriage, unlike an affair, has an ebb and a flow. Some days you feel the way you did when you first fell in love. Other days you feel dispirited, tired, distracted, disappointed, angry. Even if marriage begins with *romantic* love, it finds its continuity in *married* love, with peaks of real passion, valleys of disappointment, and plateaus of "okay" days. Successful couples know this. They have learned how to ride the waves, the crests and valleys of their marriage. When sailors hit a certain spot near the equator, they know that they may face seas that are suddenly so calm that there is no wind for their sails. They may be "becalmed"—unable to sail for some time. But they also know that this part of the ocean has its sudden squalls and light shifting winds. With skill, they can ride the wind that follows the calm.

Marriages also sail into the doldrums. These are the times when one or both members of the couple feel listless, maybe even despondent. Knowing how to talk with each other not only when times are good but even when the going is rough sees many couples through the doldrums. If a couple has a communicative relationship, they can talk about anything. This means being able to say that you are bored in the marriage, discouraged, angry, or restless. It is even possible to talk about feeling infatuated with another person. Odd as it may seem, being able to talk this frankly brings a couple closer together. There may be pain in this talk, but there is no secrecy. Even in the best of marriages, people occasionally find themselves attracted to another person. In a healthy marriage, an infatuation is merely a passing fancy.

In a marriage in which no subject is out of bounds, it is often relatively easy to solve problems that bother one or both spouses. They talk it out. They know that eventually they'll come to an acceptable solution, whether the problem is how to raise the kids, what to do about the in-laws, or where to spend the next vacation. When one or both partners in a marriage are not good at talking with one another, feelings get buried—sometimes for years. Little disappointments and angers are hidden away. Problems are not solved. When a person in this sort of marriage suddenly experiences infatuation again, but now with someone else, it is nearly impossible to talk about it. "If I couldn't tell her that she always burnt the toast," one man told me after his marriage almost ended because of a passionate affair, "how could I tell her that I thought I was falling in love?" When there is no way to talk with a mate about what might have otherwise been a passing fancy, it seems to take on a life of its own.

Secrecy is part of the excitement of an affair. The danger of discovery can be as pulse-tingling as the new relationship itself. It adds spice to life when the marriage seems bland. The affair offers a time beyond responsibility, beyond the day to day burdens of marriage, job, and family. And it is addictive, carrying with it a powerful emotional rush. As with other addictions, the rush is often followed by a sense of loss—real life doesn't seem as good. So the person is drawn to return to the source of the rush. Again, as with other addictions, there is always the feeling that it would be awful to have to give it up. The secrecy inherent in an affair carries with it not only excitement, but also fear. It is this fear that makes addicts into liars. People who are otherwise honest become remarkably skilled at lying when they fear the loss of that to which they have become addicted. Alcoholics lie about their drinking. Drug addicts lie about their drug use. Affair partners lie about their affairs.

For some, however, the lying is associated not only with excitement, but also with shame. When one woman ended her affair, she told me, "At first, I lied because I was afraid I would lose this one wonderful thing, this man who seemed to be giving me everything I lacked in my marriage. Later, I began to see that he had his faults too, and I began to feel ever so mixed up. Did I want to stay in the marriage? Was this new guy just a way of showing my husband how lousy I felt? Maybe I needed to talk about this with my husband. But now, I lied for a new reason. I was ashamed of what I had done; and still another reason—I was afraid that if my husband found out, the marriage would be over."

Lengthy Affairs

An affair may go on for as little as a month or two, or as long as the marriage itself. When a person is involved in other types of marital infidelity (such as one-night stands and philandering), the third party may be a passing fancy, or there may be a dizzying whirl of anonymous partners. In a lengthy affair there is an ever-present, although unacknowledged, third partner. Most important, the involved person is convinced that what he or she feels for this person is deep love—the kind that will last. This conviction makes an affair so distinct from what people experience in other types of extramarital behavior that it is best looked at as being on an entirely different plane. The new person takes on profound importance in the mind and feelings of the involved person. The involved person is absolutely convinced that the feelings for the new person are real and will not change.

As the sociologist Annette Lawson (1988) observed, "There are now three where there were two—the classic triangle." Sometimes there is one very tight triangle consisting of the involved partner, the partner's mate, and the third party. I use the term "third party" only to describe an unmarried third person for the following reason: if the third person is also married, she or he is in a dual role—on the one hand, as third party in the involved person's marriage, and on the other, the involved person in his or her own marriage. This means that whenever two married people have an affair, there are at least two related triangles. For example, if one triangle consists of an involved man, his wife, and another man's wife, then the second triangle consists of the involved woman, *her* husband, and the other woman's husband. Because these triangles consist of two interlocked married couples, it is simpler to look at both affair-involved people as "involved partners," and to save the term "third party" for single people.

When a married person undertakes an affair, there is often more than one motive. One woman reports that when her affair with a married man was at its most intense, she began to call the man's wife. She pretended to be an anonymous caller who just wanted to let the woman know that her husband was having an affair. At the time she did this, she was not very sure of her motives.

Later, she could see some reasons. For one thing, she hoped to shake up his marriage, so that her importance to him would be greater. For another, it gave her an increased sense of power. Now she felt that she was not only at the top of the triangle between herself, her lover, and her husband, but also at the top of the triangle between herself, her lover, and his wife. This position made her feel incredibly powerful. One man reported to me that he took his lover and his young children out to lunch one day. He pretended that she was a business acquaintance. He felt that he, the children, and his lover had now become a new unit, as if his wife, for the moment, had ceased to exist. Little by little, as the affair developed, the children felt trapped in his new relationship and unable to reveal their pain to their mother. This is one way in which people become triangulated in an affair. We will see still more examples as this chapter unfolds.

Let us now take a closer look at the affair triangle by examining the three partners in a triangle: the involved person, the discoverer, and the third party.

The Involved Partner

Nancy

Nancy married at twenty. At first everything seemed wonderful. She and Stan were deeply in love. Work was going well for both of them. They had all the things that money could buy—a lovely home, two fine cars, and frequent vacations. Although they had never discussed it before they married, Nancy was sure that it was only a matter of time before they would begin a family. When she became pregnant, she was shocked to discover that Stan was upset. He even suggested the possibility of an abortion. He said they couldn't afford the loss of income—but what he really resented, she discovered, was the change that a baby would bring to their lifestyle. They both enjoyed travel, theater, eating out, driving a fine car. In his mind the child, and the loss of Nancy's income and companionship, would spell the end of what he called "the good life."

On the surface, Stan seemed to accept it when the baby was born. Under the surface, all was not so smooth. They had never talked about her hurt when he had raised the possibility of abortion, or about his feeling that she cared more for motherhood than for their relationship. Somehow they got through this experience, she recalls, but it left her with a sour feeling. She found herself wondering how many other things they hadn't talked about before they married. Not long after the birth of their first child, and despite birth control, Nancy became pregnant again. This ended the possibility that she could soon return to work and bring in the additional income that Stan so much wanted. Although they didn't mention abortion this time, he was becoming increasingly uninvolved and irritable. He was little help with the babies, and would generally come home from work, eat, have a few beers, and fall asleep on the couch while watching TV.

At first Nancy tried to talk with him. But his answer to the question, "What's wrong?" was always the same—"Nothing." Nancy felt that she loved him and wanted, as she said, to "hang on." But it was hard. They seldom made love, and when they did, he seemed to be simply going through the motions, and she experienced no pleasure. Many times she felt a burning desire to talk about their love life, but she felt sure that the answer would be the same—"Nothing's wrong." She tried to convince herself that everything was all right. After all, they entertained friends, went to family functions, talked about the kids, even got away alone once in a while for a day or two. So maybe it wasn't so bad after all, she told herself.

One day they decided that they needed to do some house repairs. The moment she set eyes on Danny, the repair man, Nancy felt the same thrill that she had felt when she first met

Stan. He was a few years her junior, very slim and muscular. She particularly loved his deep blue eyes. Danny seemed equally attracted to her, and it wasn't long before they exchanged a passionate kiss. She thought that she could keep it "just a sexual thing, no strings," but soon found that she couldn't separate love from romance. All of the emptiness that she was experiencing with Stan was forgotten. When she was with Danny she felt so full. A smile from Danny, a word of appreciation from him, a hug seemed to sustain her. On the one hand, she began to fear that Stan would discover her infatuation, and on the other, she felt a twinge of anger that he hadn't noticed any change in her. It seemed to confirm her feeling that Stan didn't really care about her, and that only increased her passionate feelings for Danny.

Soon Nancy was making all kinds of excuses so that she could continue her relationship with Danny after the repairs were completed. Still Stan didn't notice. But he did seem to be going through another of his irritable spells, just as he had after the first child was born. He had even begun to drink—something he had never done before. One day he got so angry at some little thing that he put his fist through a wall. A few days later he happened to answer the phone. He was sure that the voice on the other end was Danny's, but whoever it was hung up. A few days later the same thing happened. This time Stan was enraged. "Are you screwing around with Danny?" he demanded. She denied it.

In the months that followed, Nancy felt ever more swept into the relationship with Danny, while Stan demanded more and more to know what was going on. The angrier he became, the more justified she felt both having and denying the affair. Finally, as she became angry with his outbursts, she found herself thinking, "What could I ever have seen in him? I must have been craving this new relationship for years." He was not the man she married, and Danny seemed the answer to her prayers. She found herself spending still more time with Danny. She imagined a new life: Danny, herself, and the children.

Soon Nancy began to notice that Danny wasn't calling as much, and that sometimes he didn't have time for her the way he always seemed to before. Stan was becoming ever more suspicious. One day he found Danny's work gloves on the car seat. He was enraged. Eventually he forced an admission from her. After she had admitted the infidelity, he told her that he was relieved that she was telling him the truth, and that he wanted her to know that he still loved her. But she was desperate to hear from Danny. When she called him, he seemed cool. It wasn't long before she discovered that he was involved with another woman—"Well, not really a woman—more a child," said Nancy, bitterly. The affair ended abruptly. The marriage didn't, although it remained very strained for a long time. For several years Stan insisted on knowing Nancy's whereabouts at all times. He often followed her, to assure himself that she was going where she said she was. One day he even showed up at her hairdresser's.

Nancy has remained in the marriage, but says that sometimes she feels like a prisoner. Stan remains suspicious but doesn't want a divorce. Strangely, he has begun to pay more attention to her. She says that perhaps this is the attention that she has always wanted. His insistence on her telling the truth, and his expressions of love and loyalty greatly increased her respect for him, although she still isn't sure that she loves him ("Whatever that means," she adds). "I guess it's foolish to imagine that I will ever feel the passion with Stan that I felt in the affair—but maybe that's the difference between a marriage and an affair." Then she adds wistfully, "Don't think for a second that I haven't felt a lot of guilt. I know that there are times Stan must have felt like having an affair too, but I'm sure he hasn't. He deserved better from me."

Leon

Leon was forty-five when he met Linda, a "thirty-something" secretary at the electronics firm that he owned. He had been married to Joanna for twenty-three years. They had a daughter aged fourteen and a son of seventeen. Leon was a self-made man. His father had been a worker in a garment factory and made a meager living. Leon was determined that he would not raise his family in poverty. He excelled in school, married while still a college student, and immediately after his graduation, began working on a master's degree in electrical engineering. Joanna left school to work full time, and Leon worked at a variety of jobs.

By the time he finished graduate school, he had already achieved several patents. One of his bosses was so interested in one of his inventions that he offered to be a "silent" partner if Leon opened his own shop. With this boost he rose rapidly in the electronics field, and was soon a millionaire. During all these years Leon continued the hectic schedule that he began as a young man. He traveled frequently to push his inventions and his company. When he was not on the road, he was at the office at seven in the morning, often working until late at night.

As the years wore on, Joanna complained that he seemed to have little time for her and the kids. Leon felt that his contribution was to be a breadwinner, and that he did it very well. It wasn't his fault that it left him little time to devote to her. He felt that they each had a life, and it was a good one. She was a wife, a mother, and a powerhouse in the community. She practically ran the PTA, as she had every other organization she'd ever been involved with. He was a successful businessman. Despite her objections, Joanna more or less accepted things as they were.

With Linda it was different. At first Leon had barely noticed her, but she had worked her way up until she became his "gal Friday." Unlike Joanna, Linda seemed to challenge him to take more care of himself. She told him that he dressed terribly, and ought to go out one day and get some new ties and shirts. He was amazed. No one had ever talked to him that way, and he was secretly flattered—so much so that he did as she suggested. When Joanna complained to him, it always seemed to be about herself, her needs. When Linda spoke to him, it seemed to be for his own benefit. Later he told me, "It was so wonderful to be taken care of—not to be the provider, the husband—just to have a free ride for once."

Leon was quite shocked when he began to feel that he was falling in love with Linda. He had always been angered when he heard of men who played around. He thought they lacked discipline and self-control. "Everything seemed so clear to me back then," he reported. Now he felt as if he were living two lives, the ever-responsible breadwinner and the young swain. He began to find extravagant gifts for Linda, which Linda greatly appreciated. It had always upset him that he could do so little for Joanna. If he wanted to get her a fur coat, or a fancy car, she would always refuse, saying, "Why waste the money—let's get something for the kids, or put it away for college." It wasn't long before he was living a double life. Joanna seemed to barely notice his absence—his hours had always been so long and erratic. After a while, though, she *did* notice, and demanded to know what was going on. Now Leon found himself violating another of his rules. He directly lied to her. It wasn't long before she hired a detective. Shortly after that she hired a lawyer, and soon there was a divorce.

Leon had never expected this to happen. He felt as if the relationship with Linda and his marriage were, as he said, "in separate boxes." Now he was angry with himself. He had shown so little fight in the divorce. He began ignoring his work and drinking alcohol in a way he never had previously. He missed his wife and felt increasingly guilty about breaking up his home. He longed for the respect that he had always felt from the children. They seemed so distant and angry now. He barely knew what to do when he was with them. And whatever he did, it seemed to be wrong.

Now there was a new complication. During the divorce action, Linda had made it clear to him that she expected that they would soon be married. With the divorce, the pressure increased, and Leon found himself less and less comfortable with Linda. He began to wonder what had attracted him to her. He began to notice little flaws. Things that he had been blind to in the heat of romance now jumped out at him. He couldn't believe that he had failed to see them before. Several years after the divorce, he broke off the relationship. About the same time his daughter, now twenty, was hospitalized following a suicide attempt. Leon was amazed at how easily he and Joanna cooperated in helping her. It was as if they had never been apart. He felt a warmth toward her that he hadn't felt in years. As their daughter recovered, he suggested to Joanna that maybe they should try again. Joanna shook her head. A little sad and a little bitter, she said, "Too much water under the bridge."

The Discoverer

Ted

Ted and Marietta had been married for twelve years. Although they married while in their early thirties, they put off having children because they were both doing well at work and wanted to establish a nest egg. As she approached her late thirties, Marietta felt that she could wait no longer, and they had a boy and a girl within a couple of years.

Although Ted was happy with their new role as parents, he also felt a certain resentment. The companionship and fun that had been so much a part of their life seemed to be dribbling away, like so much sand through his fingers. Their social life had diminished to a few friends who had also had children relatively late in life. Most of the talk seemed to be about pediatricians, diapers, day care, and nursery schools. He felt bored and a bit put off. He also felt that Marietta, once a very glamorous dresser, had become less concerned about her appearance. Often he would come home from work to find her still in her housecoat. Their love life had also deteriorated. Ted felt embarrassed that he was having so many negative thoughts. He never spoke about them, but he found himself becoming increasingly silent with her. He would often come home feeling like an outsider. Frequently he would have a drink or two, sit down in front of the TV, and fall asleep, being awakened by Marietta only in time to come up to bed. Fortunately, he thought to himself, his work was absorbing enough to see him through this dry spell. Things would get better.

Even though Ted never openly expressed his disappointment, he began to sense that Marietta was picking up on it. A little sharpness in his tone, a certain way of holding his head as he addressed her, all seemed to push her still further from him. He felt bad for her too. She was stuck at home all day with the kids. It must be unglamorous and a bit dull for her he thought, since she had held such a high-powered position before the kids came along. Although they would occasionally argue about stupid little things, they never really fought. He thought once to himself, "This must be the dog days of marriage—like the dog days of August." But they never spoke about these things with each other.

One day Ted came home to find Marietta with a new hairdo. He complimented her, and thought to himself, "Maybe she's beginning to turn around." He was pleased. A few days later, she mentioned that she felt she had put on a lot of weight since the kids came along, and asked if it would be all right if she joined a fitness club. Again, he felt pleased that she was beginning to get back into life.

But he saw no improvement in their relationship. Soon he noticed little changes in her routine that irked him. One day he came home a bit late, only to find a baby-sitter and a note explaining that she was out at the fitness center, and that there was food in the refrigerator—all he needed to do was to microwave it. Ted was hurt, but never mentioned it. The pattern intensified, and he began to worry that she might be becoming an exercise addict. She had lost a great deal of weight, and was now exercising several hours every day, even weekends. He was especially hurt when his birthday came along, and she insisted that she just had to get out and do some exercise—would he mind if they put off a birthday dinner out for another time?

One night Marietta called to tell him that she had met an old friend at the club, and would be home very late. When she arrived home at two o'clock in the morning, he was waiting at the door. He saw a second car drive away. Suddenly everything made sense. He was enraged, "You're screwing around with someone, aren't you?" She vehemently denied it. For months they argued. Every day he was more sure, and she was more insistent that nothing was going on. One night Ted followed her to the club. He saw a man in an instructor's uniform come out and give her a hug and a kiss. He thought he was going to have a heart attack. He went home, afraid that if he had stayed he might have become violent, maybe even murdered the guy. He felt that this man had stolen away his wife.

He immediately confronted Marietta: "Either stay with this man and get out of my life, or swear to me that you'll never see him again." Marietta told him that she felt very confused, and that she was frightened by his anger. Little by little, she revealed how alone *she* had felt in the marriage. He had been so inattentive since the kids were born. In the affair, she said, she felt alive again. Deep down, she knew that this was a fling, not the real thing, but it was the last thing she could tell him. Not now, when she still felt so mixed up, so unready to cut off the affair.

He was infuriated by her accusation that his distance had somehow caused the affair. He said that *she* had wronged *him,* and now she was blaming him. "Is it my fault? Is that the only thing you could think of doing if you weren't happy? To lie to me, to cheat on me? The only way to show me that you want back in is to give him up. Will you do that?" "I'm not ready to promise," she replied, "I'm still too tied up in it. If you make me promise, it will only make things worse."

Ted waited patiently for months, but agonized inside. If he saw a movie about infidelity, he had to leave. He couldn't even bear to drive on the street where the health club was located. He found himself having nightmares of Marietta having sex with the other man. At the same time, he discovered that there was still a strong sexual spark between him and Marietta. There was more lovemaking, more sexual passion than there had been in years. They were also beginning to talk about what had gone wrong in the marriage. He began to understand that perhaps she was right—maybe not that his distance had *caused* the affair, but certainly that it had hurt her deeply. Best of all, after a few weeks, Marietta told him that she had quit the club and told the other man that the affair was over. Nonetheless, for years afterward, it took very little to rekindle Ted's suspicions. Now, many years later, he says that even though in many ways his marriage is better than before, and they talk about so many more things together, feelings are different from what they were at the beginning. "In a way," he said, "I feel as if I lost my innocence."

Edna

Edna was born in El Salvador, and came to the United States when she was fourteen. It wasn't long after that she met Tony, who was twenty. From the moment that she set eyes on him, she knew that he was her "one and only." Soon she could think of nothing but Tony. And he seemed equally fascinated with her. Although her parents passed it off as a schoolgirl crush, Edna knew it wouldn't be long before they were married. Of course, there were things that she didn't especially admire about him—especially his constant flirting. Her friends told her to watch out—Tony was a playaround. Edna knew, though, that all the others meant nothing. Their relationship was stormy, often interrupted by their angry fights as she tried to confront him about his flirtations, but each time he would convince her that she was his "one and only." When Edna was seventeen she became pregnant. Perhaps because her life at home was not terribly happy, this seemed to be an ideal time to marry and start a life of her own. Shortly before the baby was born they were married.

Tony was attentive and hard working. He loved the baby, and often relieved Edna in caring for him when she was tired. It amazed her how quickly Tony seemed to slide into domestic life. As the marriage continued however, there were continuing fights about his flirtations. Many times at parties, she would find him in some secluded corner, hugging and kissing another woman. She would become furious, but he would swear that it meant nothing, it was just fun for him, but nobody would ever replace her. She accepted this, although not happily. There were particularly bitter fights when Tony stayed out very late, and she was sure he had been involved with some other woman. But still, between these episodes he seemed so attentive, so loving, so involved. She could live with it. Besides, she thought, how could these things mean anything when their own love life was so good?

By the time Edna was thirty-five, they had three children. Tony remained attentive, but she felt that something had changed. Tony had risen quickly in his work. Beginning as a "gofer" in a law firm, he had now worked his way up to a position as a paralegal. He had done so well at his firm that they gave him a scholarship, and he had completed college through years of part-time study. Now he began to complain to Edna. He told her that he felt that they were growing apart, that she had not kept pace with him. He told her that it disappointed him that she had not gone on with her education, that her English had not improved, that she was getting fat . . . there was no end to the list. No matter what she did, she seemed unable to please him.

As his responsibility at the firm increased, his hours became longer and longer. He explained to her that with his new position, if a case was up for trial, he simply had to stay until everything was ready for the next morning. That could be all night. One day she was talking with a friend and mentioned his increased work load, and how much she missed him at night. Her friend Maria wondered if maybe he had gotten himself a girlfriend. Edna was angry with her. "First of all, he wouldn't," she said, "and second, how could he? I can call him there even if he's working late." Still, a seed had been planted. She began to call more frequently—but he always answered. She began to look for things—a hair on his jacket (she found one, but he had a good reason for it), the smell of a new perfume on him (she never detected any), all the things she'd read or heard about. Nothing!

When the holidays came, there was an office party. He introduced Edna to a young woman, also a paralegal. She was about twenty-five and very attractive, with no ring on her finger. Suddenly, everything clicked. He was having an affair with this woman. That was why she could always find him there at night. That's where they "hung out." She could barely contain her rage. When they got home she confronted him. He vehemently denied it. For months she questioned him. Finally one day, in the midst of a bitter fight, he admitted it. Patty was everything his heart had ever desired in a woman. She was educated, wanted to get ahead, and was taking good care of herself. However, he said he would never willingly leave the marriage. His children and his home meant too much to him. If she wanted to leave she could, he told her. "How can I? I have no money, no job, no degree, no place to go, no way to take care of the kids." "Stay if you want," he told her, "but I'll do as I damned please." For years Edna and Tony remained in this stalemate, staying together, putting on a good show with kids and family when they weren't fighting bitterly, and surprisingly, sometimes making love. Then one day, as Tony approached his fiftieth birthday, he told her that the affair was over. Patty had left the firm and gone to another state. He had no intention of following her.

Their marriage seemed to return to its normal state. He seemed closer to her, more attentive and affectionate. But for Edna, the affair always burned in her soul. She was never again sure of him, never even really sure that he had stopped contact with Patty. She had wild thoughts—maybe she too should have an affair, just to spite him. Maybe she should tell her in-laws what kind of man he really was. The marriage lasted, but for her the passion was gone. She told a friend one day, "If I'd had the money and the education, I really think I would have left. In all these years, Tony has never once told me that he's sorry. I guess I'm just stuck."

The Third Party

You may be surprised to note that while the previous sections each contained an example of a man and a woman, in the following section we will meet two single women. In my experience with patients and in my review of people who use the Internet to talk about their experience with infidelity, I have found that if the third party is a *single* person, it is almost invariably a woman. This may explain the statistic you will often come across if you do much reading about extramarital involvements. Whatever is the estimate of marital infidelity (it ranges from 50% or more to less than 20%), there is always a higher percentage of infidelity reported for men than for their wives. The oft-used term "the other woman" reflects the common and legitimate perception that the role of the third party is mostly a feminine one. Now let us look at two such women.

Monica

Monica had just turned twenty-one and she came from a devout Catholic family, attending mass daily, and she was in her final year of college, majoring in political science. During a particularly exciting election year, she was lucky enough to be interned to the headquarters of a prominent congressman. She was particularly thrilled with her assignment because she had such deep respect for his positions on so many issues. She couldn't wait to tell her family the good news.

Perhaps because of her devoutness, perhaps because she was a bit shy, Monica had never been involved in a deep relationship with a boy, either in high school or in college. "Call me naive," she told me several years later, "but at first I didn't have the slightest idea that Jerry had a 'thing' for me." What she did sense was that he thought she brought a lot to his campaign, that her ideas were excellent, that she was a hard worker, and that he liked her. It never entered her head that his interests were deeper.

One night she stayed particularly late at headquarters, and as she was finishing up, Jerry approached her and asked if she'd like to go out for a bite to eat. It wasn't long before he began to pour out a tale of woe—how his marriage was in great difficulty, that he didn't think it could possibly last, that he had no idea what had gotten into his wife, but that she no longer seemed to love him. He told her he had never spoken with anyone about this and pledged her to secrecy.

She felt enormously complimented. Here was a man of great reputation who seemed to like her more every day. She felt honored. Best of all, he seemed to regard her as a trusted friend, a real confidante.

Although she sensed that he was attracted to her, he had never so much as kissed her. It wasn't long before he told her that he had strong feelings for her, but because of his position, they would have to keep any involvement very quiet.

So it continued for several weeks. One day Jerry asked her to stay after the rest of the staff had left. He took her hand and told her that he felt that he was falling deeply in love with her. He told her that for the first time in many years he felt young again, excited by her ideas, her enthusiasm, and her beauty. He felt that he couldn't live without her. Only then did they exchange a first, passionate kiss.

Monica was deeply touched by what he said, but at the same time she was scared. She was also beginning to feel that she was falling in love with him. She was worried, however, that perhaps this was just a "line," something Jerry said to every young assistant that came along. She made some discreet inquiries. No, there was no "dirt" on Jerry. She became more convinced than ever that he was sincere. Their relationship became more passionate, and soon they began to have sex. This surprised Monica. She could not believe that she was having sex with a married man. She felt so ashamed that she stopped attending mass, because she could not bear to confess this.

After graduation, she was to return home. Jerry told her that he could not live without her, and she felt very much the same. She made some lame excuse to her parents and stayed on in Washington. It was hard for her. While Jerry was still seen at all sorts of important dinners and charity events with his wife, he and Monica could meet only in secret. If they dined out, it was in some out-of-the-way spot where he could pass unnoticed. If they wanted to make love, it was in some sordid motel. Holidays were the worst for her, because he had to spend them with his family.

After about a year, she began to wonder why Jerry hadn't left his marriage. She challenged him. He explained that as much as he loved her, he was beginning to realize that he loved his wife as well, and that he couldn't really imagine leaving her and his children.

Monica felt devastated. She told him that it was over. A few days later, as she was planning to leave her job and return home, he called. He was desperate to see her. She refused, but postponed her return. Days drifted into weeks. She found herself driving by his home to see if his car was there. She even began calling his home and hanging up. One day, his wife answered, and she was tempted to tell her everything. Instead, she hung up.

Each time Monica felt ready to leave, Jerry would call again. A few times she saw him and they made love. Eventually she told him that each time he returned to her it only added to her torture. She felt very confused, though. She felt sorry for Jerry and the sadness of his life, and she felt bad for his wife. Not long after she realized that she was pregnant. She contacted Jerry. He was kind but distant. "Of course you'll need an abortion," he told her, "and I'll help in any way I can." "Any way" turned out to be financially. Of course, he could not be with her, because that would compromise his difficult situation. She felt she could tell no one and went through the abortion alone.

Even after that, there were months of sporadic contact in which Jerry attempted to resuscitate the relationship. Monica couldn't believe that she too was tempted to begin again. She didn't, but instead felt herself sinking into despair. One day she bought a bottle of Tylenol and started taking them in a suicide attempt. Fortunately she called a friend, who came and took her to a hospital. She was shocked to find herself crying uncontrollably with her friend. Ever so carefully, still protecting Jerry, she permitted some details to tumble out. It was the first time that she felt like her old self again. Shortly after, she returned home. To this day, she remains angry and disappointed with herself about how she behaved. Surprisingly, she bears almost no ill will towards Jerry. She doesn't believe that he was a womanizer. She simply feels that he was going through a bad time in his life, and she was there for him.

When Monica hears people talk about "the other woman," she wonders why they think it is such a glamorous role. "Looking back," she says, "I never felt like an equal—not with Jerry, not with his wife. And it's left me to this day suspicious of men—even though I don't hold Jerry responsible."

Tara

Tara reports: "I guess you would call me the other woman. I think I have been a piece of Seth and Sharon's marriage for the last ten years. Our relationship began about two years after they married." A legal secretary, now in her mid-forties, Tara has never married. "I come from a long line of divorces," she says. "On my mother's side, divorces go back three generations. I don't want to make the fourth. Several times before I met Seth I was close to getting married, but a little voice always said, 'Don't do it!—Danger ahead.'"

When Tara met Seth, a fifty-year-old lawyer with a very successful practice, things seemed to fall into place for her. They both loved theater, the opera, fine food and, as she says, "good sex." "Seth didn't seem on the make when we met—we just kind of fell into it. It wasn't long before he suggested that I move into this fine apartment, which he helps pay for. I have no illusions that he will ever leave Sharon. In his own way, I think he still loves her—and he's desperately afraid that if they ever did split, it would destroy his relationship with his kids. I have very little respect for Sharon. I think I make Seth feel good about himself, respected, maybe even pampered. In return, I get as much love as I want, and plenty of attention. I feel like he worships me.

"Sharon is a damned fool," she continues. "She is constantly critical of him. She puts him down in front of their friends. I don't think she has any real appreciation of him as a human being. That's why I can't understand why he still loves her, but I know in my heart that he does. I think I really keep their marriage together. He has a family life with her—something I really don't want—and he has romance and fun with me. Another thing that gets me: in all these years, Sharon's never once asked him a single question about where he is when he isn't with her. It's strange. I don't know whether she doesn't know, or just doesn't let on that she knows."

In many ways, liaisons like Seth and Tara's seem more a kind of "legal bigamy" than do other types of affairs. Often a man in Seth's position has considerable money and power, and can easily afford to maintain two residences. Power differences in affairs between men and single women are not infrequent. There are at least two reasons. One is, of course, the man's higher income. Because of the wage differential between men and women (there is still about a 30 percent difference) most men have considerably greater economic power than women. With this economic power generally comes higher position and rank. Most women marry men who are taller, stronger physically, and have greater incomes and higher rank in their work. So it is no surprise that if a woman, particularly a single woman, has an affair with a married man, there is likely to be this same power differential. If we add to this the fact that many men's affairs are with women considerably younger than themselves, their greater age and experience are themselves a source of power. Often it is just this power that men seek in their affairs, particularly when they are with single women.

A Few Final Words about Affairs

In this chapter we have looked at affairs through the eyes of some of the participants. I have illustrated how affairs differ from other forms of marital infidelity. The major reason is the intensity of the new relationship. For a while the affair may exist in a bubble, protected by the involved person's compartmentalization and lying and aided frequently by the mate's and sometimes the third party's denial.

In many cases, however, at some point all three members of the triangle become aware of one another's existence. The previously unsuspecting mate is confronted with information that breaks through denial. The third party who has believed that she is in a relationship with a man who will most certainly divorce his wife may become painfully aware that this will not be the case. The man or woman who was convinced that he has found his "true love" discovers that this idol too has feet of clay. Even before the moment of discovery, however, each has had a profound impact on the others' lives.

Unlike one-night stands and womanizing, lengthy affairs are most likely to arise when there are problems in the marital relationship. We can distinguish four stages that most such couples experience from the time the affair begins to its discovery. Use your journal as you think about the stages that follow.

1. *Poor self-disclosure and problem-solving*
   On the surface, the marriages of couples who later have affairs seem to be at least adequate. But upon examination, we find that one or both members of the couple find it very difficult to reveal themselves fully to their partner. The inability to express one's real feelings makes it almost impossible to resolve differences. Hurt and angry feelings can be buried for years in such a relationship. Because of this, the problems of the marriage haven't been faced.

2. *Onset of the affair*
   Poor communication and problem-solving has hurt the couple's ability to be emotionally intimate. At this point one member of the couple (it could be either) happens to become infatuated with someone, but there is, of course, no way to talk about it. The fascination grows. The affair deepens. The other mate, still believing that they are living by the rules of monogamy, is unaware of the affair.

3. *Cold rage*
   The hurt partner is still not conscious of the affair, but his or her behavior is affected by it. As evidence of the affair mounts, even if confronted, the offending mate denies it. The hurt partner believes these denials. One patient, who first suggested to me the term "cold rage," described this stage as follows: "I was irritable and incredibly moody, but I had no idea why. I had this queer feeling under-

neath, like a ticking time bomb. Even if all the evidence in the world had been piled at my feet, I still probably would have believed him."

4. *Hot rage*

The person who has until now been in denial can now no longer be. The evidence is too overwhelming. Sometimes the offending mate engineers it so that he or she must be caught. However the discovery occurs, the time bomb explodes. The pent-up hurt and rage tumble forth. Because this is a time of crisis, it is also a time of hope. Crisis, although traumatic, carries with it the potential for change. One possible change is that the marriage will improve because the couple has learned something from squarely facing a problem of such magnitude. Another is that discovery may signal the death of the relationship. In the next chapter, we will discuss some of the most frequently asked questions following discovery.

Remember

- Infatuation is not the same as mature relational love

- Secrecy and danger are part of the unrealistic excitement of an affair

- Burying small hurts and angers, rather than talking them out, is damaging to a sound relationship

❹

Is Divorce
Inevitable?

The discovery of infidelity is the source of considerable anguish. Many people report seeing their lives flash before them, as if they were about to die. They are convinced that their marriage is over. Are they correct? Does it necessarily mean that the marriage is over? No one answer covers all situations. On the surface, you might think that a one-night stand presents much less of a risk than the discovery of a lengthy affair. This is not necessarily the case. Marriages have broken up over one-night stands. Yet marriages have continued, perhaps even improved, following the discovery that one partner has been in an affair since the beginning of the marriage.

Some people report a certain relief following discovery, because so many questions are answered. One patient, Margie, was finally presented with absolute proof after months of denial. She told me, "It's so strange, but I feel so much better knowing. I really thought I was crazy before. I'm so ashamed of myself, for buying into all his lies. Now I think I'm ready to face things, wherever they take me." Once out of denial, Margie was able to face the future. Nonetheless, for many people the future seems unbearably dark during the crisis of discovery, and the past, by contrast, may seem unrealistically rosy.

Your thinking is often at its cloudiest when the pressures you're experiencing are at their height. You're not thinking clearly. Confronted by a crisis, you wish only that things could be as they were before. It doesn't occur to you that perhaps things weren't really going so well before the crisis and that going back to the way they were before would not be entirely to the good. With hindsight, you can often see that the crises you wanted so desperately to avoid have often, in the end, been important and positive turning points in your life. How often have people thought that losing their job was the worst day of their lives, only to report later that they had found much more satisfying and well-paying work?

Because the discovery of infidelity is, for so many people, a profound crisis, their first reaction is to see no good possibilities in it. However, the things that you tell yourself at the moment of discovery can easily become self-fulfilling prophecies. If you convince yourself that the marriage is over, you may unwittingly end a marriage that could otherwise be saved. If, in anger, you order your mate to "get out of my house and go live with that whore," you're telling your mate that you *want* him to do exactly that. Of course you're hurt and angry, and when you confront your spouse you'll sound that way. But try to choose the right words to express your anger. If you have just begun to suspect that your mate is involved in unfaithful behavior, sit down and have a conversation with yourself. Remind yourself, in the words of Yogi Berra, "It ain't over till it's over." Calm yourself down. Try to find good words to talk about this painful subject, first to yourself and then to your mate. Remind yourself that time is on your side, and more often than not, on the side of the marriage.

Dire prophecies need not turn automatically into truths. If you scratch people hard enough during a crisis, you'll find that, underneath what seems to be absolute certainty, there often lies considerable doubt and ambivalence. The discovered partner, absolutely convinced that his wife will never have him back, may be in shock over the discovery. It may have never even occurred to him that the discovery of the infidelity could lead to divorce. Nor may he really want one. The day before, he may have known for sure that he wanted nothing more than to end his marriage and fly into the arms of his girlfriend and live happily ever after. The day after the discovery, however, he may feel much less certain that this is what he wants. His wife, in a moment of rage, thinks she never wants to see her husband's face again or hear his lying voice. Later she may feel she wants nothing more than to get back to the "good old days" of the relationship. The "other woman" who has eagerly awaited the end of her boyfriend's marriage may suddenly find herself wondering if she really knows this man at all. Thus, after the discovery she may be much less sure than she was before that she is ready to rush into marriage, as she had earlier promised. The wife who was convinced that she adored her lover may feel entirely different as she becomes aware of all the loss she would experience if she divorced—countless hours of shared experiences, years of good lovemaking. Suddenly, she begins to notice flaws in her lover that she couldn't have even imagined the day before.

It should also be remembered that sometimes the best possible outcome of an affair is the decision to end a marriage. In the next section, we will consider both possible outcomes.

The Importance of Time

The most important rule to remember during and for some time after the discovery is: *do not rush* toward any decisive action. Discovery is a time of crisis. Like any other crisis, it can be seen as a time of grave danger, but also one of considerable opportunity. A couple who have invested years in a relationship and parented children together share a long history. As they face the consequences of all the loss that ending the marriage will bring, they may begin to look more soberly at the meaning of the infidelity, rather than focusing only on the pain of discovery. The first *meaning* they may attach to the discovery of infidelity is that their partner no longer loves them, or that the harm to the marriage is irreparable. Upon reflection, they may find a very different meaning. They may, for example, discover how far apart they have grown as a couple, and even that, deep down, they still yearn for each other. Because when they are at their most emotional they are least likely to see better possibilities, it is wise to refrain from action until they calm down.

If you are the discoverer, there is a strong likelihood that your mate is still living at home with you, even though he (or she) may be spending a great deal of time with the third party. The first thing to think about as you try to recover from your shock is that, at least up to this point, your mate is still coming home to you and not to the other person. This means that you may still have much more control than you at first thought. You may be able to use this advantage to focus on the problems *in* your marriage, and *away* from the third party. Keeping the focus on the third party will prevent clear thinking about aspects of the *marriage* that require improvement. Your mate may be in a period of intense infatuation. Don't forget that infatuation is a "high." Like any other high, it is generally followed by a crash. Feeling competitive with the third party only adds to the discoverer's pain and solves nothing.

Open your journal and fold a page. On the left side, right down your most immediate thoughts—how you're feeling right now about discovery and what to do about it. On the left side, jot down how you think you might feel later, say in a year or two, if you acted on what you're feeling right now. As you read this chapter through, you may want to go back to your list, adding to it and reconsidering some of your earlier thoughts.

A Marriage That Improved

When Kim came to see me, she was confronted with exactly this problem. Reggie was a thirty-five-year-old tennis pro who wanted nothing more than to be on the contest circuit. Although he had occasionally competed, he never felt that he could make it as a full-time competitive player. He found a job at an excellent private club, and, in addition to giving tennis lessons, he and his wife Kim ran the club store. Kim came to me alone. She told me that she was thirty-two years old, and had been married for about eight years. She and Reggie had been trying to start a family for about two years and had begun going to a fertility clinic with no success. She was convinced that Reggie was having an affair with Janet, one of his students. Kim told me that she rarely made it to the shop anymore, because she couldn't bear to see what she called "my competition." I asked her if Reggie would come in with her, but she told me they had been in therapy years before and it had been "a disaster." "In fact," she told me, "he walked out of therapy after the second session, because he felt that the therapist favored me. I kind of agree with him—the therapist did seem much more in sympathy with me."

I suggested that, since Reggie would not come, it would be important for her to imagine that he was in the room, and even better if she could take his side along with her own. This might be a very different experience for her than her previous therapy, I suggested. Before, she had felt very supported by the therapist, but found that Reggie had been turned off because he felt attacked. Now, thinking in this new way, she began to sense that Reggie might be feeling upset about their inability to conceive, and that his interest in this young woman might well be an ego boost for him. Further questioning revealed that, despite the fact that he was sometimes seen at the club bar with Janet, his hours were still regular. He came home on time and did not seem changed in any other way, except maybe a little more "down." She also began to realize as we spoke that she and Reggie had never really talked with one another about the stress and disappointment connected to their attempt to have a child. I made two suggestions to Kim. The first was that she have a good talk with Reggie about their attempts to conceive. The second was that she return to the store and begin to enjoy working together there with Reggie, as she always had in the past.

Kim returned to the next session greatly relieved. Armed with her new ideas, she had gone home and had a "heart to heart" talk with Reggie. She told me that, instead of beginning by accusing him of having an affair, she began by telling him that she was wondering how he was feeling about their fertility problem. He revealed to her that it was really getting him down. For one thing, he told her, he didn't feel as much of a man—somehow, even though the doctor had been so reassuring, he couldn't get out of his mind the idea that maybe it was his fault. He also told her that he felt a real loss of interest in making love. "It's like it's a chore now, a real production," he told her. "It used to be such a great bond between us." He also told her that he found himself thinking a lot about how disappointed he was with himself because he wasn't good enough to be a full-time competitive player.

Kim told me that she felt very good about this conversation. It was the first time in a while that she felt they had really talked intimately. She also had followed my suggestion and returned to the shop. "I really took a good look at Janet, and I can't imagine what he sees in her. I think he would be a fool to leave me for her.

I took your advice and didn't talk about Janet—but, to be honest with you, I'm still positive that there's something going on between them, and I hate it. Isn't it time to confront him?"

I suggested that she think first about having a conversation with Reggie about how to get the spark back in their marriage. At our next meeting, she reported that she and Reggie had a long talk about how focused they had become on getting pregnant. It seemed to be almost all they talked about now, and especially since they weren't getting anywhere yet, talking about it only made him feel worse. "Maybe," he had told her, "we should stop worrying about it for a while, and start having some fun again. It's all you ever talk about, and it's a real downer." Although at first it hurt to hear him say this, Kim told me that, deep down, she knew he was right.

They promised each other not to talk about "the problem" for a while, and see if it helped. Kim told me that they had gone out a few times, were being more affectionate with each other, and making love again, now with some real passion. "Still," she said, "I can't get over the feeling that there's something going on with Janet."

At the next meeting, Kim told me that things were really improving, but that she was upset because, one evening after they made love, Reggie told her that he knew she had been uptight about Janet, but that it was nothing, really. He admitted to hugging and kissing her. "Partly," he had told her, "because she was so unhappy in her life, and it brought her some comfort. Partly, I guess, because it made me feel like a man again, that I could really be there for a woman." As Kim explored her own feelings, she realized that she was hurt, but also relieved to find out that she wasn't so crazy, that something really had been going on. She did demand that he stop any contact with Janet. Tearfully, she told him that she just wanted things back the way they were before. Reggie told her that he wanted it *better* than it had been before. He had begun to feel that the love was going out of their marriage, that it was getting to be less fun and companionship than it had been at the beginning.

It was a week or two later that Reggie teared up one day and told her that he had something really hard to talk about with her. Kim was frightened but ready to listen. He told her that he'd been more intimate with Janet than he'd admitted before—in fact, he'd had sex with her. Kim was deeply hurt. Reggie told her that the only reason he felt safe telling her now was that he knew, in his own heart, that the affair was 100 percent over. He told her that nothing like this had ever happened in their marriage before, and he really felt ashamed that he had lied to her.

Kim continued to feel hurt and suspicious for several months. She and Reggie had a few tiffs because he felt that she was watching his every move. Kim explained to him that it was only natural that she was suspicious—after all, he had lied to her a lot. Reggie seemed to accept this and was more accepting and reassuring when she had occasional bouts of suspiciousness. At the same time, she began to notice that he was courting her more, and she was very receptive. They began to talk about their courtship and the early years of their marriage, remembering the good times. This reminded them that they had married for good reason. She also found herself beginning to go out of her way to do little things that she knew meant a lot to him. When he won an important tournament, she got him a shirt labeled "champ," and took him out for a fancy celebration dinner.

About a year after Kim ended her therapy, she called to let me know that everything had been going wonderfully, and, best of all, she was pregnant. The affair was now a distant memory. "We really trust each other so much more now," she reported. "I feel that we've been able to talk about so many things, good and bad. I think our marriage is affair-proof now."

Kim and Reggie were able to see that the life crisis they had gone through while trying to conceive had taken its toll. They agreed that their courtship and early marriage had been, for the most part, happy, but they also realized that they were not communicating well. Because of that, they had begun to drift apart. They agreed that they needed to get beyond the infidelity, and they understood that to do that they had to be able to speak openly about both positives and negatives in their relationship.

Why is it reasonable to expect that Kim's prediction is correct, and that there will not be another affair?

- This was a first affair.

- She was able to keep her hurt and anger under control.

- There was a full admission that there had been an affair.

- There was a sincere expression of remorse.

- There was a mutual decision to improve communication.

- They could see a clear reason why the affair had occurred.
- Each of them expressed a willingness to change.
- They did not stay focused on disputes about the third party.
- He accepted her suspiciousness undefensively.

Ambivalence

When people feel ambivalent, they harbor both negative and positive feelings towards a person, thing, or situation. In a state of ambivalence, you feel simultaneously drawn in opposite directions. Neither Kim nor Reggie suffered much ambivalence. Although Kim was hurt and frightened by Reggie's infidelity, the thought of ending her marriage never entered her mind. Reggie also had never really thought about leaving Kim. Many people, confronted with evidence of infidelity, are much more ambivalent. They find themselves overwhelmed by questions. As they first search for and then find answers to their own ambivalence, they come to grips with whether or not there will be a marriage after the dust stirred by the affair settles.

Understandable Concerns

I strongly advise my patients to take some time to think carefully about their ambivalence. I suggest that they try hard not to engage family and friends in discussion about what has happened and what to do about it. In the midst of the hurt that accompanies discovery, the injured party is likely to cast the involved partner in the role of villain. Often, the ambivalence that accompanies the hurt is ignored, and the spotlight shines brightly on the hurt and anger. Later, the marriage may go on to heal, but friends and family with whom the hurt person has spoken may not forget so easily. This can be a source of subsequent problems. As one patient told me, "I really regretted having spoken so angrily to my mom about Charlie. She was all love and support when I was hurt and angry, but she also started to attack everything about him. Then I felt hurt for both of us, and I was angry with her for taking over my battle. Charlie and I made it through, but I think she still considers him the bad guy, and I resent it."

Some Questions to Consider

The questions that follow refer first to the discoverer only, then to the involved person, and finally, to both. These are all questions that I have heard many times from my patients. They are also themes that occur frequently on computer bulletin boards that deal with infidelity. These questions and your answers to them may help you to see more clearly how you will resolve your own ambivalence.

Discoverers

Is it my fault if my mate is having an affair?

NO! Your mate had many options short of an affair for solving whatever problems he or she perceived in the marriage. Do not let anyone blame you for the deceit that you have suffered; but while the affair is not your fault, it *is* important that you think about how your actions, as well as your partner's, may have contributed to a readiness for the affair. There is a difference between being told (in effect), "It's your fault that I was a liar and a cheat," and deciding together that there were issues that needed to be talked about that had not been well resolved.

I am so confused! One day I think I am ready to kick him (her) out, the next I desperately want to keep the marriage. Is this normal?

It is quite normal. Feeling this way is evidence that you are experiencing the ambivalence that I described earlier. People who are struggling with ambivalence often find it helpful to ask themselves whether they are ready to continue their lives regardless of what their ultimate decision is, to stay or to leave. Once you break out of the feeling of being trapped, it becomes possible to think more clearly and less emotionally. Now you are ready to explore your ambivalence more objectively. At that point, the following question becomes important.

**My wife was unfaithful, but now she's back. She claims that her affair is really over, and she wants the marriage again. I find myself wondering if she's back because she really loves me, or is she back because she doesn't want to lose the package—you know, the house, the kids, the position in the community? I think I may be accepting her back for the same reason. Is it a good idea for either of us to stay for the "package"?

Marriage means more than the husband-wife relationship. You may have raised children together. You probably have developed important relationships with one another's families. If you are like many people, you have a network of friends that are really as much your couple's circle as they are friends of either of you as individuals. The loss of a home can be a very traumatic experience. People often become wedded to a place, even a favorite spot. One man told me that when he began to consider leaving during his wife's affair, his thoughts turned to his favorite easy chair and how he loved to sit in it at day's end and look out at his garden.

If you are thinking about the package, it suggests that you feel that with it comes a certain security that you hesitate to abandon. This may well be a sign that you are beginning to reconsider the wisdom of your affair (if you are the involved party) or that you are ready to put aside your hurt (if you are the discoverer) and reexplore the positives of your marital relationship. If you believe you are returning because of the "package," be very sure that you undertake a very serious examination of what led to the affair. If you can talk about it and agree upon and carry out the necessary changes in your relationship, you will both be winners. If you come back *only* for the package and without any meaningful change in your relationship, there is, unfortunately, a good chance that there will be another affair. Staying in your marriage because of the easy chair overlooking the garden will not, in all likelihood, justify your staying in the long run.

My husband wants me to engage in sexual acts that I find disgusting. Now he claims that his affair was because of my refusal to do these things. Is this the real reason for his infidelity?

Most sex therapists will tell you that "good" sex is consensual sex between two adults. If your husband wants a sexual experience that is obnoxious to you, you might talk openly with him about other sexual acts that neither of you has explored that might bring pleasure to you both. If, despite continued attempts, he cannot be budged, you need to consider two possibilities:

1. His demands are unfair, and he makes you feel as if you are not an equal partner but merely a sexual object for him. If this is the case, you need to think carefully about the possibility that this is simply the tip of the iceberg, and that there are many other ways in which you also are made to feel more like a thing than a person. Should this be the case, you may need to clearly confront this, probably with a good marital therapist.

2. You may sense that there is some fairness to his request, and that you would benefit from speaking alone with a competent therapist about your own sexual inhibitions. This may be of great help to you. Many women have discovered in the course of therapy that early in their lives they experienced some event or series of events that have caused serious sexual problems later in their lives. I have treated several women who discovered experiences such as sexual abuse in their childhood that left them unable to achieve orgasm. Through therapy, they were able to overcome their inhibitions and achieve a mutually pleasurable sexual relationship with their husbands.

My wife recently admitted to an affair of well over a year, after thirty years of what I thought was a happy marriage. She now claims she is "back for good." I am not sure that I can ever feel safe with her again, but I am very sexually attracted to her. After holding off for a while, I have started to have sex with her again, but I feel very mixed up about it. By being sexual with her, am I confusing myself even more? Will I fool myself into staying for the wrong reasons? Also—if I decide to divorce her, won't I have been leading her on as well?

One frequent sign of the death of a marriage is a feeling of disgust at the idea of sexual involvement with one's mate. The presence of sexual interest is not a sure sign that the marriage will last, but it suggests that there may still exist a real potential for a return to an increasingly safe relationship. Probably one of the problems in your marriage through the years has been a poor level of communication about important feelings. Given this, you may be tempted to keep your confusion to yourself. You would do better however to be very honest in describing your feelings to your wife in all of their complexity. This would probably open communications considerably, perhaps more than they ever have been. The better your communication becomes, the more resolved you will become about your confusion. There is a strong possibility that such conversations will lead to a real improvement in your ability to be intimate with each other. By intimacy I mean much more than sexual relations. Intimacy is the ability to share all kinds of feelings and ideas, "good" and "bad," with a feeling of complete safety. I put these words in quotes because very often what we fear our partner might see as very bad may lead to a particularly productive conversation.

Is my husband, who had an affair, really telling me everything? I am very curious about what kind of sex he had with her, and especially if he did things with her that he doesn't do with me. Is my curiosity unhealthy?

It is not unusual for offended mates to want to know what went on sexually during an affair. Some patients report that they believe they need this information, and press until they receive it. In many instances, they subsequently discover that finding out may have satisfied their curiosity, but hurt them in other ways. As one woman said, "Knowing the gory details left me with pictures in my head that I didn't want or need. I found myself comparing my breasts with hers, my short, curly hair with her long, beautiful tresses. It was like there were three in the bed. I regret having asked." I suggest to my patients that they turn their attention instead to how they would like, as a couple, to improve their own love life. Most find that making the shift away from the third party and back to their own relationship, helps to restore a sense of closeness and intimacy.

Curiosity includes, but also extends beyond sexual issues. Here are some of the questions most frequently asked:

- Was he (or she) better looking?

- Better in bed?

- Better endowed?

- Was I talked about or made fun of?

- Was it one of my friends?

- Were intimate details of our or our children's lives talked about?

- Did mutual friends plot with you to protect the affair?

As to those questions that involve the appearance and sexual skills of the third party, the above answer holds—most people find that learning about these matters does little to improve the couple's relationship or love life. As to the others, they involve the violation of privacy. For most people, it is these violations that are most serious. They need to be talked about, often for the protection of the injured party. For example, if a woman discovered that her husband has cheated on her with her best friend, she needs to know this in order to protect herself from further hurt from the former friend. By the same token, if you know that things were shared with the lover that shouldn't have been, you will need to figure out together how to repair the boundaries around your most intimate life together that have been broken. Talking about these painful topics strengthens the discoverer's faith in the returning mate's sincerity.

My husband has had a number of affairs through the years. Some I know about with certainty, because I caught him red-handed. Others I suspect. He has never really come clean. He certainly has never said he was sorry. I feel dead in the marriage, but I stay. Am I staying only out of fear?

The fact that you asked that particular question suggests that you already know the answer. If you feel that dead, and that with so many chances to come clean, he never has, chances are that you are now staying out of fear. Women in particular are likely to experience more fear as they contemplate divorce. Women generally suffer financially in a divorce, particularly if children are involved. You may have very justifiable fears. This would be a very good time to consult with a competent therapist to begin to explore your fears. You should also consider talking with a lawyer so you have some understanding of your legal situation. As you do, you will begin to develop a sensible plan that will give you, in all likelihood, the courage to leave. In many communities there are also available groups, generally called "Women in Transition" groups, where women find support as they contemplate or go through marital separation. There is an interesting irony here, though. It is possible that, as you strengthen in your resolve to leave, he may once again very much want to continue the marriage. Should that happen, you will have a new opportunity to explore what has gone wrong with the marriage but with more power on your side.

My husband swears to me that he has ended a lengthy affair. It is now several months, but I get all kinds of phone calls from people whose voices I don't recognize, telling me that he's still fooling around with her. We also get a lot of hang-ups on the phone. Am I a fool to believe him?

No, not necessarily. If his schedule is once again reliable and you know where he is and what he is doing and if the marriage appears to be improving significantly in other respects, it is entirely possible that he is telling the truth. Put yourself in the position of the other woman for a moment. Imagine what she is experiencing. Chances are that she believed that your marriage was on the rocks and had reason to believe that, in time, he would divorce you and marry her. Imagine her hurt and disappointment. Frequently, it is only after a person feels jilted that this kind of behavior, sometimes called "stalking," begins. In part, it is an attempt to maintain some kind of contact, however limited, with her "boyfriend." In part, it is an act of jealousy. In part it is an attempt to stir up trouble between you. If you and your husband can talk honestly about the impact of the stalking on your lives, you can then begin to figure out together how to approach this painful problem. Filtering all of your calls through a telephone answering machine for a month or two may be helpful. Usually, if nuisance calls are not answered, they eventually will stop. At times this is not practical, and it is necessary to involve the phone company. They will usually ask that you make a formal complaint to the police. Then, they will track the calls. But be careful—they then expect you to prosecute the offending parties. Stalking may take other forms as well. The stalker may follow the former lover by car. Patients report the jilted partner jackknifing her car in front of his or bumping him in order to force him to get out of the car to talk. Many stalkers call the stalked party at work, figuring that there may be a greater likelihood of their getting through, or possibly to humiliate the former lover. Many couples report to me that the act of joining together to face the problem of stalking has been an important aspect of their reconciliation. As one woman told me, as she and her husband worked to stop a constant flow of phone calls, "I began to feel that we were on the same team again. It was a very healing experience. I could tell by the way he took part in it that he had really ended the other relationship. It let me know how bad he felt about what he had done to our marriage, and how much he wanted to be back with me."

My husband has had several extramarital experiences. I don't know if they were affairs or just playing around. He has never fully disclosed what they were about to me. I haven't had sex with him in a number of years, so the question of sexually transmitted diseases never entered my mind. Now he says that he wants to resume a sexual life with me. I told him that without testing, I would never feel safe. He refuses to be tested. What do I do now?

Your question indicates that your husband has, to this point, never been honest with you about his extramarital experience. He is being no more honest about the possibility of a sexually transmitted disease. If you resume sexual relations with him, would it be because you also want to, or would it be more to service him? If it is primarily for his gratification, what is your motive? If it is a matter of maintaining the security that marriage affords you, you may feel forced to give in and resume sexual relations. If you do so, it would be urgent that you insist that the rules for "safer sex" be followed. I put these words in quotation marks to remind you that there is no such thing as absolutely safe sex if the person has been involved in unsafe practices.

I am impotent because of a medical problem. My wife claims that this was the cause of her affair. How can this problem be resolved?

Many men face impotency problems. For most, they are a cause of considerable sadness. Many men feel that they have lost their masculinity with the loss of erectile ability. In most of the couples whom I have treated who are faced with this problem, the wife's affair is not a direct result of the impotence. Wives in this situation reveal in therapy that their complaint is his loss of interest in bringing her pleasure. Another reason such women report is their husband's depression following the development of impotence. Many men who believed that their own sex lives were over have discovered a renewal of their own interest in sexuality as they once again became interested in bringing their wives pleasure. It should also be remembered that it is often worth your while to have additional medical consultations if only one doctor has told you that there is nothing more that you can do. There may be others with a different approach that might be more helpful. If there is medical agreement that there is no hope for physical improvement, psychotherapy is strongly recommended to deal with the depression.

My wife admitted an affair of several years' duration. She tells me that it is definitely over, and I am inclined to believe her. She has apologized many times over for the hurt she has caused me. She tells me that she can understand how violated I must feel. I appreciate all this. But every time I've asked her if she doesn't feel guilty about the affair itself, she has avoided the subject. Recently we had a heated argument, and she told me that she didn't regret the affair at all. She says it was a beautiful time in her life. Can she really regret hurting me and still not show any remorse at all about the affair?

People in the throes of an affair are intoxicated with it. One patient described it this way: "It's like being the star of a great romantic movie. It has great sex, constant attention, and mystery. What could be better? I felt adored in my affair." Later, after the affair was long over, she could see it in a somewhat different light. "In my marriage, I feel loved—the kind that lasts, even though it has its ups and downs. But to be honest, I really miss being adored, even though I knew deep down it could never last." People seem to have the ability to remember the affair very warmly, perhaps even wrapped in a romantic fuzziness, in which details that were not so positive are forgotten. This does not necessarily mean that they are pining for their lost lover. It is more that they miss the adoration and the excitement. If your marriage is, by any other standard, a happy one now, I would urge you to avoid obsessing about why your wife can't renounce the good feelings that the affair brought her. Instead, I would suggest that you keep the focus on making sure that the marriage you now have is satisfying for both of you.

My wife's affair ended only when I discovered some love letters on our dresser. It is months now that it's over, but I can't get the idea out of my head that it would have gone on forever if I hadn't caught her. Is this a common problem?

I'm not exactly sure from your question whether the problem you're asking about is your fear that if you hadn't caught her it would still be going on, or the phenomenon of getting caught. Let's tackle "getting caught" first. In the novel *Crime and Punishment*, Dostoyevsky describes Raskolnikov's compulsion to be caught in his crime. I suspect that this is not a problem that professional criminals experience. For them, crime is their life and their livelihood. There are no issues of conscience. By contrast, a child who has been involved in drugs is likely to leave little bits of evidence about because, deep down, he is in some conflict about his drug use. The loving parent discovers this evidence and confronts the offending child. In the end, it is a relief for the child to be found out. This is sometimes characterized as a call for help. Leaving evidence of an affair around is also a call for help. Frequently, the offending mate expresses similar relief at being found out and even sees the hurt person's discovery and confrontation as acts of love.

As to your fear that the affair would have lasted had you not discovered it, it is more likely that you discovered it because you were out of denial, and because she was ready to be discovered. It is true that sometimes people are ripe for discovery when they are ready to end their marriage. Even in this instance there is often a sense of relief, because the need for deception has ended. However, since you report that your marriage has improved, the meaning of the discovery seems to be that it was time to put energy back into the marriage, rather than to put an end to it.

Involved Partners

It is several months since I ended my affair. I know I did the right thing. So why am I so sad about ending it, and why am I still so obsessed with my former affair partner?

It is only natural that the ending of an affair is accompanied by a sense of sadness, loss and obsession. The ability to make deep attachments is a very important quality. We wouldn't be much as people if it we could just say to ourselves, "easy come, easy go." Chances are that you and your affair partner planned, or at least fantasized, that you would be together forever. You may feel guilty that you have hurt and disappointed the other party. You may miss the good times, even though you have decided to return to your mate. Time and distance are the great healers. It is very important (although very difficult) to resist checking up on your former lover. But if you do, you may breathe life back into the affair, bringing more pain to both your mate and your lover—as well as yourself.

If you have accepted the idea of a moratorium, observe the time limit you have set, and work to see if your marriage can succeed without the distraction of another emotional involvement. Trying to do both will only confuse you more.

My wife just discovered that I am a compulsive womanizer. I guess you'd say I have a sexual addiction. But I really care about her and the kids. None of my involvements have lasted for any length of time—most of them just a night, while I was on the road selling. None of them have had even a spark of romance. I don't know what makes me do this. She told me to get out, but the last thing I want is a divorce. Is there any hope that we can get beyond this?

In chapter 3, I described sexual addiction. Sexual addicts generally have very poor self-esteem. They also are generally incredibly skilled at denying what they are doing, both to themselves and others. The fact that you are now able to give a name to what you have been doing is significant. As with any other addiction, admitting that you are addicted and feel no power over your addiction is a painful but necessary first step. Your question does not indicate whether you have admitted openly to your wife that you have this problem. By admitting it not only to yourself, but to others as well, you show a readiness to get the help that you need. You should immediately seek assistance from a therapist who has already demonstrated competence with this problem. The issue of therapy selection is dealt with in depth in chapter 10. Such a person will probably also refer you to a group that helps people with sexual addictions, if there is one available in your area. The books by Carnes and by Earle and Crowe (see References) can provide a great deal of insight into this problem. As your wife sees that you are sincerely pursuing therapy for yourself, she may then be willing to begin marital therapy together with you. It will be important for you to remember that she has been deeply hurt by all the lies that covered your addiction. You will need to be remarkably sensitive to all of her misgivings about staying married to you. Your ability to listen supportively will be important to her. She may also be terribly afraid that she may have contracted a sexually transmitted disease from you. Both of you should be tested as soon as possible.

My former lover has been stalking me. Some of the things that have happened have been pretty scary. She has left messages on my voice mail at work threatening to reveal "who I really am" to my boss. We used to make love on my boat, and she still has the keys to it. One day I went to work on the boat and found her locked in the cabin. She wouldn't leave until I talked to her. Then she threatened to tell my wife that we had a liaison on the boat. I hesitate to talk to my wife about this stuff. I am afraid it will only remind her of the bad times and also that knowing how crazy my ex-lover is might scare her. I'm also afraid that if my ex-lover called her and told her that we had gotten together again, my wife might believe her. What should I do?

It is obvious that your former lover feels betrayed by you and would like to either get you back or extract her revenge on both you and your wife. By withholding important information from your wife, you are repeating the pattern of lying that was such an important and hurtful part of the affair. It is clear that you believe that you are protecting your wife by withholding the information. There is also evidence that you believe that not telling her protects you as well. The truth is that when you withhold information, you are lying. Eventually, the truth is likely to come out. Even if it doesn't, the danger of its discovery will hang over your marriage like a dangling sword. Imagine your wife's hurt should she discover that she has been deceived yet again? When I tell my patients about a "better marriage," I remind them that a good marriage is, above all, an honest relationship. Believing that you must be your wife's protector must be a remarkable burden for you to carry alone. Think of how liberating it would be to know that, whatever the remaining issues about the affair are, you may face them together. Patients frequently tell me that, having faced the fallout of the affair together, they began to realize that they could face anything together.

My affair has ended. My wife has demanded to know whether I was having an affair, and I have denied it. She keeps hounding me. Friends have told me to keep my mouth shut, that eventually it will blow over. Is this good advice?

Although it might seem to be common sense to stonewall it until she stops asking questions, it is actually a very poor policy. For one thing, the worst is over. Her questions indicate that she is ready to know (if indeed she hasn't figured it out already). She can't let go of the question because she needs you to validate that she was not crazy to be suspicious. When patients come to me suspecting an infidelity, I ask them whether they know the difference between paranoia and rapanoia. If you look in the dictionary, you won't find "rapanoia," but I can't think of a better way to distinguish this feeling from paranoia, which is the unfounded and delusional suspicion that others mean you harm. *Rapanoia* is the opposite—the appropriate suspicion that someone *is* harming you. I tell my patients that if there is reason to believe that their fears are founded, they should hold onto their rapanoia for as long as they need it. They will not rest easy until they know that the terrible suspicions and fears that they have harbored are not the result of craziness, but the breakthrough of denial.

Years ago, Alfred Hitchcock's film, *Gaslight*, described how a person can be driven to the point of madness by another's deception. In that film, Charles Boyer's deception of Ingrid Bergman was ended only when a policeman cleverly deduced that the flickering of the gaslight which she had noticed was the accidental result of Boyer's dishonesty. It was Boyer's plan to drive her mad so that he could inherit the money he believed she possessed. I mention this long story because it well help you to understand that your deception has the accidental power to make your wife doubt her own perceptions, and, therefore, her sanity. Unless that is your plan, it is urgent that you admit to her what she so strongly suspects, or perhaps even already knows. There are generally two issues which stand in the way as people contemplate confessing:

1. *Confessing will only hurt my wife (husband). She (he) is very weak, and this will shatter her (him).* This protectiveness suggests that your marriage is not one of two equal adults, but one in which one has considerably greater power and responsibility than the other. If this is indeed the case, it's probably one of the things that spurred on the affair. People who are overresponsible in their marriages can tire of this burden. When the opportunity presents itself, the affair seems to be the perfect antidote to this exhaustion. By not revealing the affair, the whole issue of dependency and overresponsibility is kept under wraps—so even if *this* affair has ended, there is a strong likelihood that others will follow. The act of revealing the affair, in the end, puts you on an equal footing and could produce meaningful changes in your relationship. You may even feel that you can reveal things in the relationship that have made you uncomfortable for some time. This process will probably be difficult for both of you. There are many things that need to be talked about, not just the affair, but the marriage itself. As your communication improves, your marriage becomes increasingly affair-proof. A major reason for telling the truth is that continuing to lie deprives you both of the best marriage you might have.

2. *Confessing will hurt my former lover.* I described earlier the loyalty that many affair partners feel toward their former lover. They feel that they have already hurt the third party enough. Why inflict more damage? On rare occasions, this is true. It would be unwise to reveal the name of the third party if you believe your mate capable of causing harm to the other party. However, this is extremely rare. For the most part, what the hurt partner craves is validation, followed by an intense desire to return to an improved marriage.

My affair is over, but I am still having a problem—to paraphrase Shakespeare: "To tell or not to tell?"

On the surface, your question may seem identical to the one above, but it's not. In the above question, the wife is asking for validation. From your question, it would appear that your affair is undiscovered. I assume that you also believe that it is unsuspected. In many instances a mate harbors a subliminal sense that something is awry. If you sense that this is true, then the above reply is applicable. In instances where it is certain that the mate is unsuspecting, I have occasionally seen situations in which the decision was made not to reveal the infidelity. The person who makes such a choice places a burden on him- or herself. The person must do, alone and unaided, all the work that the couple might otherwise do. He (or she) must examine alone what created a readiness for the affair, and must then, without arousing the mate's suspicion, begin to suggest the kinds of changes in the marriage that would insure that another affair will not occur. They must, of course, also make changes in their own marital behavior. Patients who take on this task report to me that they feel they and their marriages have changed for the good. The unfortunate side effect is that they always harbor the nagging fear that the infidelity will somehow come to light at a later time, causing even more damage.

Both Partners

Can I ever trust (in the case of the involved partner, be trusted) again?

Trust is regained only slowly. Remember, the loss of trust is a major feature of the post-traumatic reaction that was described in chapter 2. It takes a while to begin to feel secure again. Every good day that you have as a couple is a move toward increased trust. To the degree that the person who has been hurt feels reassured by the offending mate, and patiently heard out when suspicions return, trust begins to rebuild. Another sign of the restoration of trust is that both husband and wife can now realize that there were unacknowledged marital problems that had increased the likelihood of an affair. A couple that faces these issues with mutual responsibility is on its way toward healing. However, if the hurt person becomes aware that there is another infidelity, or that the marriage has not improved in terms of communication and mutuality, trust will be further weakened. Repeated violations of trust will lead to further decline in the relationship. In the event that the offending mate was a compulsive womanizer, his wife will require additional proof that he is taking personal responsibility for this problem, and seeking help to recover from it. Womanizers, generally speaking, will only face their problem if they fear the loss of their marriage. Thus, its discovery is the ideal time to demand that he get help. If he sincerely does this, that too will build trust.

Would the quality of my life improve if the marriage ended?

There are four questions that can help you to think this through:

1. What is the best thing that could happen if I stayed?

2. What is the worst thing that could happen if I stayed?

3. What is the best thing that could happen if I left?

4. What is the worst thing that could happen if I left?

One patient, Louise, was faced with a husband who had, over several years, three affairs, each of some length. He never admitted them until they were well over, and showed no remorse. Her answers to these four questions were:

1. Best if I stayed: Things would stay about the same— maybe I might force him to get help—but I've tried before and never succeeded. Probably, just stay the same.

2. Worst if I stay: He could keep doing this over and over, and whatever is left of my self-esteem will plummet.

3. Best if I leave: Maybe I would feel better about myself. I might even meet a decent man—I think I could do better.

4. Worst if I leave: Knowing him, he would probably do everything he could to screw me in a settlement. How would I take care of the kids if that happened?

As Louise thought about it, she came to the conclusion that it was not safe to leave while the children were still preteens, but that she could not survive forever in this marriage. She decided to use the years until the children were grown to develop new job skills. This gave her a goal and made it easier for her to survive from day to day.

Josh, another patient, had been in an affair for several years. In therapy, he came to accept the probability that he would not end up marrying the woman with whom he was involved. He had begun to feel, however, that even if his new relationship did not work out, and he was left, as he said with "no safety net," that he still might need to end his marriage. Here is his "best-worst" list:

1. Best if I stay: I guess I could just go on this way—but I hate the lying. I've tried to talk with Margaret [his wife] until I'm blue in the face, but I don't think she'll ever change.

2. Worst if I stay: That it would just stay the way it is, and that I would keep lying or one day just get caught, maybe "accidentally on purpose."

3. Best if I leave: I would stop hurting Margaret—I know I'm not being fair to her—and maybe find some happiness for myself.

4. Worst if I leave: This is a killer. I adore my kids, and I think I'm a model father. If I leave, they might really be disappointed in me, see me as the bad guy. Worse still, I wouldn't see them every day. I hate the idea of being a Sunday father.

Josh decided to begin talking about divorce with Margaret. Much to his amazement, he discovered that she had suspected an affair, and had been thinking of discussing it with him. Once he knew that she was already suspicious, he felt reasonably safe in admitting it and apologizing for the lying. They decided to get some therapy together. In the course of it, they were able to accept mutual responsibility for the failure of the marriage and to mourn its death. They were also able to begin to plan a divorce that was fair and protected their children.

$$\hookleftarrow$$

Should I stay for the sake of the children?

There is an abundance of evidence that divorce is bad for children. Given this, it is highly ethical to consider very carefully its impact on them. It is not unusual for both husband and wife to be thinking about this problem as they experience the consequences of infidelity. Unfortunately, although each may be thinking about it alone, often the two do not discuss it together.

We know that at least the first two years following separation have strong negative effects on children. By comparison with children in intact homes, more of them experience academic decline, behavioral problems, and a variety of emotional problems. Thus it would seem at first glance that divorce will have only bad consequences for children; but the situation is more complicated. The effects on children of living in a tense, angry, loveless environment can also produce profound problems for children.

Earlier in this chapter, I described how Louise made the decision to stay with her husband until her children were grown. During therapy, she talked often about her wish to shield the children, as much as she could, from her dissatisfaction with the marriage. In order to do this, she decided that she needed to remind herself that she was powerless to change her husband, as she had tried to do for so many years. She was able to say to herself, "He's really not such a bad guy. It's just that he is not the right guy for me, and never will be. What gives me the right to force him to change?" Once she accepted this, she found that there was a remarkable reduction in their fights. She also found herself much less likely to make bitter and sarcastic remarks to the children about "your father."

Josh, on the other hand, came to the conclusion that he could no longer tolerate his marriage. He showed his concern for his children by taking the step of honestly talking with his wife first about his affair, and then about how to move toward a fair and honorable divorce. This amicable ending offered dignity to Josh, his wife, and their children. It also helped them to escape a home that had been filled with hurt, anger, strife, and dishonesty. About a year after the separation, I had an opportunity to meet alone with their children, Beth, who was by then fifteen, and twelve-year-old Jimmy. Both agreed that they had hated the squabbling that they had witnessed for so many years. The separation had been very hard at first, but now, seeing each of their parents alone, they both felt that they were now getting the best of both parents. "It's weird," said Beth, "but I see each of them in such a different light now. Mom is so much more laid back, and Dad is so much less serious and critical all the time."

Both Louise and Josh thought carefully about the consequences of divorce on their children. In many cases, people do not. They divorce in rage, often causing their children the continual pain of having to take sides. As one child told me, "It's like this: If I say something nice about Mom to Dad, he thinks I hate him. And the other way around with Mom. So, I've just learned to keep my mouth shut."

Certainly the best possible case is that the affair ends, the couple learns from it, and family life greatly improves for all concerned. Children are the beneficiaries of such a resolution. Since many infidelities do not end marriages, there is reason to believe that a slow, patient consideration of the meaning of the affair may result, in the end, in a reconciliation.

Failing this, it is important to ask yourself if you can remain in the marriage in a way that does the least possible damage to your children.

If neither of the above is possible, a good divorce may well be in your children's best interests.

The Search for Meaning

The psychiatrist Victor Frankl was imprisoned in a Nazi concentration camp during the Second World War. During his imprisonment, he tried to fathom why some inmates were able to survive this unbelievably demeaning and degrading experience without losing their own humanity, while others crumbled. He came to the conclusion that those who survived emotionally were able to find some form of meaning in this most ununderstandable of circumstances. For some, this took the form of a promise that they made to themselves that at war's end, they would devote their lives to telling others what had happened in the camps. Others survived by determining to help others in the camps, even as they themselves were suffering so. Out of his observations, Frankl wrote the book, *Man's Search for Meaning* (1975). Once we have found meaning in the most trying events that may beset us, we can then face them with the survivor's vigor.

Each of the questions we have examined is a search for meaning. In the end, the meaning that we find is not in the objective facts alone—what the discovered person did and with whom—so much as it is in the meaning that the discoverer makes of these facts. The discovered person also will be able to make clear decisions about where the infidelity will lead by finding its meaning for him- or herself.

I stressed earlier that time is on your side as you struggle through the meaning of the infidelity and its discovery. Many people in the end can acknowledge that the discovery, as painful as it was, served as a wakeup call to reexamine and reorganize the conditions of their marriage. If a couple makes this profound struggle, they grow closer as they face their pain. They discover that they have increased in maturity. They have become better friends. They have come close to the brink and realized the peril beyond the cliff. They don't ever want to come that close to the edge again, and they resolve that their marriage will be forever changed. The major transformation will be a level of communication and honesty that they had never even imagined was possible.

Sometimes discoverers realize that, despite the fact that the offending mate wants to maintain the marriage, they no longer can. Unlike the decision to stay together, ride the infidelity through and come to a better marriage, the decision to end it is a solitary one. One patient, the wife of a philanderer, put it this way: "My husband has come to me, once again, to tell me that he's sorry, that he didn't mean to hurt me. After twenty-five years of marriage, it came to me in a flash. I had heard him say this too many times. It was as if for the first time, I saw things clearly. In the past, each time he confessed and apologized, it was the first time. Now, I could see the chain of too many admissions and apologies. It would never change. Never in all these years was he able to say, 'I have a problem,' nor would he ever. So, finally, I admitted to myself that I could never change him, and he would not change himself. This means that, for my own protection, I must leave."

The involved partner may also find meaning in an affair. When I work with people who are in the midst of an affair, I attempt, as I described earlier, to indicate the unlikelihood that their affair will become a long-term relationship. I help them to understand that they must consider their motivation for the affair very carefully as they face the possibility that they may end their marriage.

After Janine's affair, she had to face just that possibility. I had first seen Janine and her husband, Murphy, several years prior to her affair. At that time, Janine very much wanted her marriage to work. But she could no longer bear his silence. She felt that he gave little to the relationship. She did everything she could to bring Murphy to his senses. She became depressed, but he didn't express much concern or give her the support that she so craved. She tried anger, but it only angered Murphy. She threatened divorce. At that point, Murphy decided that therapy was not for him, and withdrew. Janine came for a few more sessions, in which she tearfully admitted that she could not bear the marriage, but she found the thought of divorce equally unbearable. She said, "I know that inside of that shell, there is a good man. I am determined to find that man." At that point, she also left therapy.

Several years later I received a call from Janine asking to see me as soon as possible. No sooner had she seated herself than she said, "I think I'm in love." As she described her lover, I expressed my feeling that she had found a new Murphy, another diamond in the rough. We explored how she happened to become an "amateur jeweler." As she described her parents' relationship, she soon acknowledged that she had learned diamond cutting from her mother, who devoted her life to attempting, as she had so often told Janine, "to bring out the best in Dad." As Janine heard herself say this, she laughed. "I guess I'm doing with Murphy exactly what Mom did with Dad!" Despite this, when I attempted to explore the similarities between her relationship with Murphy and with her lover, she couldn't see it.

Eventually Janine asked for a separation. Now she had Murphy's attention. Much to her shock, once it was so available, she found that she didn't especially want it. It wasn't long after the separation, however, that she could admit that she had been repeating her old pattern, this time with her lover. It was strange, she told me, that as she felt herself closing out the marriage, she also suddenly became aware of all the little faults in her lover that she had until then ignored. She decided to separate from Murphy for a while, but to discontinue her affair.

For several months Janine saw neither Murphy nor her lover. In therapy, she continued to explore the messages that she had learned in her home as a child. She realized that she didn't want the job of "fixing" anyone. After a while she decided that she wanted to explore the marriage again and asked Murphy to join her. They remained separated for close to a year, then began to date each other. One day, Murphy suggested, "Why don't we go steady again, as we did in high school, and let's see how it works out." She said, "Sounds good, but you've got to get your own head straight first—I've retired from the helping game." Murphy decided to have some therapeutic sessions for himself. In therapy, he realized how much like his father he had become. He had always resented his father's neglect of his mother and sided with his mother when she and his father fought. He had made a thousand promises to himself that, when he married, he would be a much better husband than his father had ever been. He was shocked to realize how closed down he had become, so much like his father. He worked on how to feel alive and connected in a way he never had been before. Soon he and Janine got back together. Both agreed that they had learned much from the pain of the affair.

In this chapter, we have examined the *meaning* of the discovery of infidelity. We have come to see how important it is to focus on the marriage itself, away from the infidelity. We have explored many of the questions that discovery produces. This traumatic event can, in the end, be a source of profoundly meaningful change. Certainly divorce is not inevitable. In many cases, once issues raised by the affair are resolved, the result is an improved marriage. In some instances, the affair reveals the need to end the marriage. The saddest couples that I treat are those who simply remain in a loveless marriage, forever plagued by the infidelity but never using it as the powerful force for change that it can be. In the next chapter, we will explore the emotions that have so much power over us as we face a crisis.

Remember

- The discovery of an infidelity is not always the death knell of a marriage

- It is important not to make quick decisions when an infidelity is uncovered

- Admission and remorse are crucial if a relationship is to survive an infidelity

- Time and the search for meaning are potent ingredients in surviving infidelity

Feelings That Help and Feelings That Hurt

The intense emotions that you experience as you move through the stages from discovery to recovery are a potential source of both pain and of growth. You can learn to use your emotions to help you grow and change. It is not always so easy, however, to sort through the jumble of feelings you are experiencing and find a useful meaning in them.

If you are like most people, you think of blame, shame, guilt, and anger as negative feelings. You want to rid yourself of these feelings as rapidly possible. This certainly seems understandable. Because nobody is better at escaping from emotions than an alcoholic or a drug addict, examining how they deal with emotions is instructive. Recovering addicts tell us that a single slip can spiral them back into addictive behavior. Rather than facing their disappointment about the slip, they feel so ashamed of themselves that they begin to binge, which brings them a brief respite from their unbearable shame. Relapsing, however, only serves to increase the very sense of shame they are trying to deaden. The next thing they know, they are deep into another episode of active addiction.

Imagine, instead, that even the most seemingly negative emotions might have as strong a positive as a negative effect. Terry, a heroin addict, explained to me how he had kicked his habit many years ago and never relapsed. "One day I found myself in the dark hallway of a tenement building where I had gone to cop some heroin. Something went wrong, and I passed out. When I did, the guy I bought the heroin from robbed me and stripped me of my clothing. He probably left me for dead. When I awakened (a needle still stuck in my arm) and realized what had happened, I was overcome by rage at the guy and fury at myself. How could I have done this to myself? How long could I go on lying to my wife and my boss? I felt so ashamed that I wanted to kill myself. How close to death would I have to come before I got the message? Later, I realized that this experience was a gift. It was the warning I needed. I went into a rehab program and never relapsed. Not that I haven't been tempted; but each time I am, I think of the shame and self-hatred I felt that day, and it reminds me that I never want to feel that way again. That stops me in my tracks."

Terry's story indicates the intense power inherent in what we might first think of as a negative emotion. He experienced a burning sense of shame. He hung his head in the face of what he had done to himself. He stopped blaming others, and took direct responsibility for his own behavior. Terry's sense of shame changed his life, because he put it to good use.

Wouldn't it be wonderful if you could know that at the end of all this pain you could emerge transformed? In this chapter, we will consider both the harmful and useful aspects of emotional states, so that we can focus energy on the useful power inherent in what at first might seem to be even the most negative feeling.

Idiot Lights and Negative Feelings

Years ago, automobile manufacturers came to the conclusion that the American public was incapable of reading the array of dashboard meters that until then had adorned most cars. These invaluable little devices told drivers a great deal about the state of their vehicles. Were they running a bit hot? Was the battery charging properly? Was the oil pressure correct? In their place, Detroit created a dashboard with little red lights. These lights told drivers that the car was on the verge of boiling over, that it was out of oil, that the battery was about to die. People called them "idiot lights" because it would take an idiot not to understand their meaning. Of course, in their oversimplicity, they deprived the consumer of a wealth of information that could have prevented the damage that was so close at hand.

I became aware of the connection between idiot lights and emotions only by accident. Helen was seeing me because of her rage at her husband's affair. She told me that she felt unbelievably ashamed of herself. "I should have known," she cried. "Everyone must see me as such a fool. I can't bear to show my face in public. I am so angry at the people who knew and never told me. No matter what my husband does or says, I could never find it in my heart to forgive him." Her list of shame and blame was endless. I did everything in my power to help her to get beyond her hurt so that she could take some positive actions, but I couldn't budge her.

The drive from Helen's home to my office was close to an hour. One day she came in quite agitated. "What does it mean," she asked, "if the red light is on in the car?" When I asked how long it had been on, she told me, "Almost the whole ride here. I was afraid to stop." I told her I thought it meant (sadly, it turned out that it did) that she had burnt out her engine. We called for someone to pick up the car, and Helen decided, as long as she was there already, to continue her session. As we talked, we saw how much her life was like her behavior in the car that day. Her emotional red light was on almost continually. Rather than learn from it, she ignored it. Instead, she experienced the sense of panic that seeing the red light can cause. Then she felt trapped in her panic and unable to think clearly.

There are two separate elements to an emotion. One element is the gut feeling. When we are angry, we see red. When you are upset, you may feel it in the pit of your stomach. When you're humiliated, you may blush. The second element is the thoughts that accompany these feelings. The psychiatrist Aaron Beck (1988) has spent his career studying cognitive psychology—the relationship between what people think and how they feel. Common sense tells you that you become upset because something negative has happened. For example, you might experience a problem with your car this way: "The car broke down—my day is ruined."

Beck writes that it is not the *fact* that the car broke down but the way you *think* about it that causes the problem. The first thought that may come to mind is that the day is ruined. It is this thought that may unleash a flood of feelings—anger, frustration, perhaps even panic—"Oh dear—now I'll never be able to get to that appointment—what will happen then?" The more you spiral into this pattern, the more negative emotions you'll churn up. You may find yourself looking for someone to blame: "I told her to get the car checked yesterday." Or we may blame ourselves: "I'm such an idiot. I can't even take care of my own car. I never do anything right." Each of these thoughts produces still more emotional discomfort, leaving you feeling still less in charge, still more upset.

Recent study of how the human brain works strongly supports Dr. Beck's observations. If you scan the brain of a person who is gripped by an obsessive and upsetting thought, you can actually see the brain become agitated. The more overcome people are with emotions, the poorer their thought processes become. But you can literally *change* your mind, rid yourself of the bad feelings, and free yourself to think more clearly. For example, you might say to yourself: "It's not such a big problem—I'll call a tow truck. Meanwhile, I happen to have a good book with me, I might as well do a little reading to get my mind off this." Very obsessed people are often treated with medication to help quiet the obsessions. But what if it were possible to get the same result without medication, simply by teaching the patient to think differently? The psychiatrist Jeffrey Schwartz (1997) trained highly obsessed people to distract themselves in this way and could track changes in their brain waves as they learned to calm themselves. By talking to themselves in a new way and by learning to calm themselves, patients who had suffered from excruciating obsessions learned to be free of them.

Your mind tells your brain what to tell your body to do. The human brain is very obedient. If you tell yourself that your life is a catastrophe, your brain will tell your body to go into catastrophe mode. Your heart will beat fast, you'll sweat, your muscles will tense. If you remember the symptoms of trauma that were described in chapter 1, you can see the dramatic effects of what you think on the way you feel. Your whole body responds to how you see your situation. So it isn't surprising that the feeling that you are in a catastrophic situation can make you sleepless, cause sudden outbursts of anger, or make you jump at the slightest sound.

Imagine your negative emotions as red lights. Of course, when you are in pain you may need some time to cry, to scream, to release the pain you are feeling. Sometimes you may need desperately to let off steam. But remember, those painful feelings are a source of tremendous energy for positive change. As long as you stay in this pained state, you cap up this powerful source of energy. The red light stays on, causing a constant flow of useless, nonproductive energy. If it stays on for long enough, it will burn you out. How long can a person withstand endless guilt, endless shame, endless anger?

Use your journal now to make a list of all the angry and hurt thoughts that you have been experiencing as a result of the infidelity. Next to each item, write down what you think are the negative consequences of your thoughts on your behavior and even on your physical health. If you are the discoverer, you might focus on the natural human tendency to place blame on someone for the pain you are experiencing. You may be blaming it on yourself, your mate, or the third party. Use your journal to sort our your feelings. You may find yourself blaming yourself. If you are, try to break down your thoughts into two categories:

- endless self-blaming that leads you nowhere and makes you feel worse

- accepting mature responsibility for some of what went wrong in your marriage

If you are the mate who is involved in unfaithful behavior, you may also be blaming yourself, your wife, or the third party in ways that hurt and do not help. Use the same scheme to note your feelings.

Dealing with Anger

Through the years, there have been two opposing ideas about how to handle anger. One is that you should "let it all hang out," and that to do anything less would be dishonest, perhaps even dangerous to our health and well-being. The other is that you should keep it to yourself because of its power to hurt others and perhaps yourself. Each of these theories is troublesome. If you let it all hang out, you find that, despite your expectation that you'll feel relieved, you often feel angrier, more ashamed, and more uncomfortable after your outburst than before. If you hold it in, it can take its toll in depression, addiction, or physical illness. So either holding it all in or letting it all hang out can keep the red light on.

Staying in a state of gut anger has still more unfortunate consequences. Anger begets anger. The more angry you let yourself be, the more angry you become. You can become so angry that every time you think of the object of your anger, all you can associate that person with is anger. I have treated people who have become so angry with a child or a parent that they have simply stopped any contact with that person. They tell me that they can no longer think about the person without feeling overwhelming anger. The irony is that, even though the angry person may believe that they have solved the problem by ending contact, what happens in fact is that the angry feelings remain, with enormous power to produce ever more anger.

Anger also brings forth a number of unwanted responses in the person with whom one is angry. If you express gut anger at someone, that person may simply display equal anger at you. Or the person may defend against your display of anger by becoming distant from you. This can lead to an almost unbreakable cycle of anger—anger at self, anger at the distancing person, leading to still more anger and still more distance, or an endless explosion of mutual anger. Clearly, such a cycle prevents people from using their anger in a productive manner. If your red light is on, you can be sure that your anger, shame, or guilt will be nonproductive. How can we unleash the profoundly positive and productive change that Terry experienced when he awakened from his drugged state?

How to Make Emotions Productive

If letting it all hang out doesn't really work, and holding it all in doesn't either, what should we do with these powerful emotions? The psychologist Harriet Goldhor Lerner, in her book *The Dance of Anger* (1985), describes the particular effects of anger on the lives of women. She points out that the anger that women feel is often the result of feelings of powerlessness. Women pay a price for the open expression of anger in our society. They learned from childhood on that they are to nurture, serve, and soothe. They also learn that the direct expression of anger is "unladylike." They often learn to "deself." This occurs, explains Lerner, when women "betray and sacrifice the self in order to preserve harmony with others." A deselfed woman turns her anger inward, and can endlessly wonder what she did wrong that led to her husband's affair, rather than examining the relationship itself. There are a number of ways that women learn to express anger that, as Lerner says, "do not work in the long run. These include *silent submission, ineffective fighting and blaming, and emotional distancing.*" Each of these modes, she reminds us, is a way of avoiding the direct and productive expression of anger. She also observes that the effect of poorly managed anger is most often to keep a situation, however poor, from changing. A classic example of this is the wife of an alcoholic who may beg, threaten, and cajole her husband but never learns to take care of her own needs. These same behaviors are often part of a woman's response to her mate's infidelity, with equally poor results.

Men also get caught up in the negative effects of anger. Emotionally and physically abusive men are often caught in a cycle of gut anger that they feel unable to control, anger that may even erupt in violence. Because most men are taught early in their lives to "be a man," they block themselves off from their feelings. For many such men, almost all feelings can be expressed through only two modes: anger and sex.

In order to turn a negative feeling or thought into a usable form you must make the following important distinction:

- **emoting** (showing the raw emotion) has negative and unpredictable consequences—you may have an occasional "win," but, in the long run, you lose.

- **reporting** (describing what you are feeling in calm, clear words) opens up communication and invites change.

Learning to report what you are feeling, rather than emote it, has two important consequences. First, it calms you down. As you find clear words to report what you are feeling, you will notice that the tension in your body is releasing, you're thinking more clearly, and you feel a sense of power that your gut emotion had deprived you of. Second, you discover that you now have the power to be heard and taken seriously. It is easy for the person you are angry with to dismiss your *emoting* as a sign of craziness—but clear, nonattacking reportage of your feeling makes that charge impossible.

In my previous book *Bridging Separate Gender Worlds: Why Men and Women Clash and How Therapists Can Bring Them Together* (1997), the psychologists Carol Philpot, Gary Brooks, Roberta Nutt, and I describe an interviewing technique that helps couples hear each other. If one partner is upset, the person asks to be interviewed by the other. The following instructions are adapted from *Bridging Separate Gender Worlds*. The interviewee is asked to:

- Speak in "I" language, not in finger-pointing "you" language.

- Report what you are feeling—don't emote it. Don't blame the other person, but carefully describe what is happening inside yourself.

The interviewer is given these instructions:

- Listen attentively to what your partner is saying. Don't interrupt.

- Listen for the feelings that lie beneath your partner's words.

- Look directly at your partner.

- Be aware of what your body is saying to the other person—for example, nodding agreement or disagreement.

- Resist the temptation to answer back.

- Stop after a few minutes to put into your own words what your partner is saying. Even take a stab at telling them what you imagine they might be feeling.

- Draw you partner out as completely as you can. Lose yourself in you partner's feelings. Put yourself completely in your partner's shoes.

When couples are able to communicate in this manner, they become empathic with each other. *Empathy* is the ability to enter into the feeling state of another person. In my years of helping troubled couples, I have begun to feel that empathy is even more enduring and valuable than romantic love. When I work with a couple who tell me that they love each other but fight continually, I tell them that I am more interested in whether they are "in empathy" than whether they are in love. No instrument has more power than empathy to help people change their behavior toward one another. When you know someone empathically, you are often willing to change not because it is demanded of you, but because you can now feel for the other person. Often people have no idea of the pain that they unwittingly inflict on one another.

Debra and Charlie experienced such a change. Debra, a forty-ish secretary, had discovered close to a year ago that Charlie had been having an office romance. By the time she admitted to herself that it was going on, a year had already passed. She arrived at my office with Charlie, an executive in a large insurance firm. Tears streaming down her face, fists clenched, she paced the room, angrily gesturing at him. "You bastard. You and that whore—you made a fool of me. Was there anyone in your f—ing office who didn't know? Was I the only jerk in the world who didn't know? You are such a liar. I'll never let you get a divorce, but I'll never let you forget what you did, either."

Charlie sat in stony silence, white faced. After about ten minutes, he said, "Can't you get off of it? I know she still works in the office, but I don't even say hello to her. I swear it." "Sure, that's what you tell me," she shot back. Charlie suddenly got up out of his seat, as if to leave. "Doc, there's no way I can prove to her that I stopped. I told her a million times. She just can't get off of it."

I asked Debra if she could take a minute or two to calm herself, and then talk to him about her own feelings, using "I" language. I reminded Debbie that when you speak using "I" language, you are forced to put into words how you are feeling, rather than attacking the person you are addressing. At this point, Debbie began describing what she had experienced during the affair. "You don't know how bewildered and scared I was during the months that you denied that you were involved with her. I felt as if I was going crazy. Friends began to tell me that you were playing around, but I refused to believe them. When I found out, I felt destroyed. I felt so empty and alone. I was ashamed to talk to my friends who had warned me, because I felt I would look like such a fool. I began to search for every bit of evidence that I could find, and I found plenty, but it didn't bring me any relief. I felt dirty for sneaking around, sniffing things out, being a detective. I can't stand what this has done to us. I hurt so much."

As Debra spoke, I watched Charlie's face change from a stony mask of anger. Now his attention was riveted on her. He began to tear up as he listened. As she finished, he reached across to her and took her hand. "I never realized how much I hurt you. I am so sorry for what I put you through." Over several weeks she was able to regain a sense of safety with Charlie. At that point, he was able to share with her some of the things that he felt had begun to sour him on their marriage and made him ready for an affair. They talked together about her overinvolvement with her children, her parents, and her siblings, to the point that he felt closed out and alone. Because they were no longer attacking, they could at last hear each other. Out of that good hearing came mutual empathy. Later, both agreed that the turning point in their marriage was the moment that they felt truly able to feel for one another.

This would be a good point to use your journal to explore how you are expressing anger. Think of times that you have been angry as you faced either discovering or being discovered. How did you express that anger? Can you make a clear distinction between times you were able to report it instead of emoting it? Can you think of some current angry feeling and find a good way of expressing it clearly to the person you are angry with? Is there some other person with whom you could talk out your anger if you feel that you can't be heard by the person you're angry at?

Blaming

Blame is another action that heats up emotion and prevents problem-solving. Blaming, unfortunately, is not only something that other people do to you. It is also something that you may do to yourself. It isn't unusual for a person to think, once the initial anger at discovery has abated, "What did I do that made him (or her) want someone else?" Because blame is such a strong emotion, it tends to hurt more than it helps. When you blame yourself, you feel like beating yourself up. When you are in this frame of mind, it is all but impossible to think clearly and constructively about your situation.

Blaming the third party is equally unproductive. People often say, "She stole my husband away." But people can't be stolen. If people leave a marriage, they do it on their own two feet. Talking a great deal with each other about the third person keeps a couple from talking about their own marriage and where it is going. When I begin working with a couple after the discovery of an infidelity, one of the first things I tell them is: "This is a no-fault office. We aren't here to cast blame, but to figure out what has gone wrong and how and whether it can be repaired."

Blaming your mate is equally understandable, but equally useless. I have seen marriages end when they didn't have to be-cause the offending mate felt that the other person's inability to let go of blaming made it impossible to talk about real problems in the marriage. The fear of being blamed can also inhibit a mate from talking about heretofore undisclosed personal problems that may be associated with extramarital behavior, because they may be seen as excuses. For example, Ben, one of my patients, resisted re-vealing to his wife that he had become addicted to cocaine. He ex-plained to me that, until he discovered cocaine, he had always been a quiet, introverted, and very conservative person. Through a business associate, he discovered not only cocaine, but also a wild lifestyle that he had never even imagined but was quickly drawn into. "She'll divorce me the minute she hears. I must have already told her a million lies to cover up the crazy life I've been living." Yet, when he finally admitted it to her, she was able to see that both the cocaine and the call girls were part of his addictive behavior. She agreed to stand by him under the following conditions: that he would enter a treatment program, undergo testing to be sure he had not acquired a sexually transmitted disease, and that he would end his coccaine habit and his extramarital involvements.

Accepting Responsibility

There is something to be said about the possible benefits of experi-encing blame and the feeling of shame that often accompanies it. When we feel blamed, our first reaction is to become defensive. However, there is a positive side to blame. It may lead us to the mature acceptance of responsibility for an improper act. Accepting responsibility enables us to undertake a course of change. In order to do this, we must somehow get beyond the immediate feelings aroused by the act of *being* blamed. Often the best way to accom-plish this is to listen from the point of view of the blaming person. "I hate you because you've lied to me. You're nothing but a liar." The recipients of these accusations feel like either cringing or fighting back. But if they can get beyond the pain of hearing these words and thinking "I only wish she (or he) would shut up," and instead focus on the pain *they* have created, then new possibilities for change open up. Now the hearer can say (if not publicly, at least inwardly), "Yes, I did that. I accept full responsibility for it. It was my choice—I could have done differently. And I can feel the pain I have caused."

Shame can also have both negative and positive consequences. The average criminal exhibits the most primitive level of shame. If you watch the evening news, you will generally see some recently discovered scoundrel being led out of some building. You will notice that he has covered his face with his hat, his hand, or a newspaper. He is embarrassed and ashamed—if not about what he did, at least about being caught having done it. He may also feel some pain for the shame that he's brought to his family and others close to him. Often the shame passes, and when a new opportunity presents itself, he repeats the same behavior. In some instances, this sense of shame acts as a kind of brake on our misbehavior. A patient of mine, a lawyer, broke a number of laws connected with his work. He was caught and, amidst great publicity, was tried, convicted, and finally jailed. It was at first his sense of shame that made him promise to himself that he would never again do anything so shameful. He could not accept the humiliation that he felt when he knew that people were pointing at him and talking about the things that he had done, nor could he face the humiliation that he had brought upon his wife and children. He swore to himself that he would never again do anything that would put himself or his family in such a position again. Nonetheless, he told himself, "Everyone does it—it's no big deal. It's just that I was the unlucky one who got caught."

It was only during his time in jail that he began to think more deeply. It suddenly occurred to him that he felt deeply shocked and pained, as he said, *inside* of himself, for what he had done. "I have betrayed the trust that was placed in me, and, if I'm honest with myself, I must admit that I've stolen from my clients." He was now experiencing the deep remorse and grief that comes with healthy guilt. It is this sense of guilt that has the capacity to produce deep and lasting change.

In this chapter I have focused on the range of feelings that the discovery of infidelity can stoke up and how you can harness the energy of these feelings to produce positive change. In the next two chapters, you'll see how using emotions in a productive manner helps to clarify the relationship and leads to better communication and problem solving.

Remember

- Your emotional red light is a signal to organize your thoughts so you can express them clearly

- Describing your feelings calmly makes you feel better and more in control

- Blaming others or yourself doesn't help

- But learning to accept remorseful feelings can produce healthy change in relationships

- Learning to "interview" you partner will increase good communication

- Deep change in relationships comes from feeling empathy for each other

Trust

The loss of trust is the most painful result of the discovery of infidelity. When trust is lost it's hard to sit down and talk about what has happened, what it means to each of you, and what the future holds for your marriage. Many people report that their attempts to begin talking are disastrous. What may start as a quiet conversation can become a heated argument within seconds. The story that Bill and Kathy told me in therapy provides a useful example.

Bill and Kathy had been married for fifteen years. They had two children. Bill was a construction worker, and Kathy, who had been a legal secretary before the children were born, now considered herself a homemaker. Kathy had always seen Bill as a kind and dutiful husband, although not much of a talker. However, she had begun to sense that something was changing. Bill was less attentive and even more quiet than usual. He seemed irritable about little things that had never bothered him before. He was coming home much later than usual, often with alcohol on his breath. This puzzled her. Bill had never been much of a drinker. No matter how hard she tried, Kathy couldn't get a clear explanation from him. The more questions she asked, the more irritated he became.

A friend suggested that he might be involved with someone. Kathy was angry with her friend and didn't speak to her for weeks. However, the thought gnawed at her. A few weeks later, she found a lipstick that wasn't hers on the front seat of the car. Bill first denied knowing anything about it, and then said, "Maybe I picked up a hitchhiker." At this point Kathy became enraged. She knew that this was out of character for Bill, and insisted on finding out more. It wasn't long before he admitted that he had strong feelings for someone, but he insisted that it was just a passing fancy and that nothing had happened. Kathy was amazed at her reaction. "It was as if something snapped," she said. "I never believed that such sounds could come out of my mouth. I was screaming and cursing. I hit him. I hit him so hard he cowered." With it all, Bill said he wasn't sure he wanted to end the marriage, and, at the suggestion of a friend, they entered therapy.

When a couple like Bill and Kathy comes to my office, the first thing I do is to help each person understand why the pain is so great at this moment. I point out that the person who has discovered the infidelity is in shock, and feeling betrayed. Until this understandable feeling can be fully accepted by the mate who has been involved in an affair, there will be little hope for change. Using the description of trauma described in chapter 1, I explain that the discoverer is in the midst of a reaction to the trauma of discovery and that there are steps that the couple can take to begin the process of healing. The first step is to begin to heal the immediate wound. Imagine the pain of discovery as if it were a wound on the skin. If it kept getting reopened, it would become more infected. Until the irritation was ended, there would be little hope that the wound would heal. Continued lying scrapes the wound of infidelity over and over.

But it isn't unusual for the affair-involved partner to scrape the wound by denying the infidelity, even though the evidence is overwhelming. Sometimes the person denies out of the fear of the legal consequences of telling the truth. Sometimes it is the fear of the spouse's wrath once the whole truth is told. Sometimes people are afraid that once the admission is made, questions will be asked whose answers might only make things worse. Often it's the fear of being forced to stop the hurtful behavior—even though the person may be very unsure about wanting a divorce. In Bill's case, several friends knew about his affair. In fact, a couple of them had been involved in it, one by providing a place where he and his girlfriend could meet and another by lying to Kathy when she had checked on Bill's whereabouts one day. Both friends had advised Bill to keep his mouth shut, no matter what. When he finally admitted his "passing fancy," his friends urged him to say no more than he had to. This isn't at all unusual. Many people get advice from friends, lawyers, or the media that strengthens their resolve to deny the truth. The fact that it is the advice most often given does not mean that it is good advice.

In most cases it's only after the truth is told that it becomes possible to communicate once again. Lying creates an all but impenetrable barrier. If you are lying, every time you speak with the person you are lying to, you check to see whether the other person is buying it. If you are being lied to, even if you are not yet absolutely sure, you may very well have a vague sense that something is wrong. Many people report that once they've been told the truth, they understand that at some level, they knew all along. But along with the relief comes hurt. As one woman told me, she found out something she really didn't want to be the case.

Both partners need to understand that restoring trust won't be easy. The worst fears of the unfaithful mate may be quickly confirmed. The first response that most people have to an honest admission is very emotional. At the very least, discoverers may cry, shout, or throw things. At the very worst, they may attempt to strike out physically. Often rash statements are made—"You bastard—this is the end—I'll never trust you again—the next time you'll see me is in court."

Preparing for the Confrontation

- If you are the involved mate—and you are not yet ready to make an admission—think about what stands in the way for you. Use your journal to list your own worst fears about your mate's reaction. Can you think of things you could do or say that might ease this difficult conversation?

- If you are the suspecting mate, can you imagine and journal what you might do to prepare yourself for the conversation that you're sure is to come, so that it generates the most light and the least heat.

When Bill admitted what he had done (at least a piece of it), Kathy's enraged response at first convinced him that the marriage was over. Weeks later, as he began to regain her trust, he realized that she'd just been expressing her shock and hurt.

Often the unfaithful person's first response to a mate's anger is to be defensive. People do this in different ways. One is to continue to deny. "You're nuts—you're paranoid. Nothing's going on." Another is trying to stop the anger: "Just calm down—get a grip on yourself—cut it our. Yes, I did it—now let's forget about it and just go on." Still another is to justify their behavior: "You were never really there for me when I needed you, and that's why I went elsewhere." Each of these responses will only intensify the discoverer's pain and sense of isolation. The best thing for the discovered person to do is to listen carefully to the pain of the discoverer and accept it. There will be time later to begin to talk.

Most people who act unfaithfully didn't intend to hurt their partner. They frequently aren't at all sure why they did what they did. Because they're so unclear and often also ashamed, their attempts to explain seem hollow and false. Therefore, any attempt to explain the infidelity at this point seems to the discoverer like an excuse. Not every infidelity takes the form of affairs. There may be some still unrevealed secret—perhaps sexual addiction, perhaps the person is ready to come out as a gay, lesbian, or bisexual. It is only after the pain of discovery has begun to lift that the couple can begin to talk about what preceded the infidelity, and how—if at all—the situation that led up to the infidelity can be corrected.

What Can Help

The advice that follows is equally important whether or not the unfaithful partner believes at that moment that he or she wants to stay in the relationship. It's important for both of you to realize that if you stay together, you'll need to improve your communications with each other. If you decide to end your relationship, it will still be important to communicate honestly in order to arrive at a reasonable agreement. If you have children, you should understand that divorce won't end your contact with one another. There will be many times in the years to come when your ability to respect each other will be vastly important to your children. There will be school graduations, religious events, weddings, and important medical decisions—the list of times you will be called upon as parents, even though you may no longer be mates, is lengthy. Many people also report that if they can talk honestly about the failure of their relationship in a nonblaming way, they each leave it with increased understanding. They can then enter new relationships with the benefit of what they've learned.

The restoration of honest communication must first come from the person who has acted dishonestly. To do this, there are two tasks that must be accomplished. The first deals with clearing the air by admitting what has happened. The other is accepting responsibility for the pain caused by the lying that is always part of cheating. To achieve these two goals, the involved partner must, in his or her own words and in as much detail as needed, make two statements. These statements acknowledge the reality of what has happened and open the way for honest communication:

1. **ADMISSION:** Yes, I have been involved with another person (or persons).

2. **REMORSE:** I understand that, because of the many lies that I have told you, I have hurt you deeply and destroyed trust. (Note that the remorse is not about the act of infidelity, but specifically about the lying.)

These two statements convey a powerful message. They tell the discoverer that his or her feelings of betrayal are real, not merely imagined, and that they are understandable. Admission and remorse can also have a profound effect on the unfaithful partner. True remorse changes people. If you reach deep inside of yourself and take responsibility for the pain you have caused, you are not likely to repeat the act that triggered your remorse. Who would want to feel such pain again?

Preparing for Admission

- As the involved partner, use your journal now to write down what you are ready to admit to. If you are leaving things out, why are you doing so? Can you honestly say you are ready to stop the offending behavior? If not, are you ready to admit that you don't want to stop?

- As the mate who knows that a confrontation is coming, use your journal to write down your worst fears. What can you do to be sure that your partner can be honest with you? What techniques have you used to deal with other stressful events in your life that might help you through this?

- For both partners: Try hard to focus on the great good that can come from honest talk, as frightening as it may seem.

Write down some of the possible good that could come from this conversation.

However for many people neither of these steps is easily taken. Let's return to the case of Kathy and Bill. Bill began by admitting that he had feelings for his coworker, Jeannette, but denied that things had gone any further. Kathy didn't fully believe him because he was still acting so strangely. So she kept on checking things like his car mileage, telephone bills, and his beeper. It soon became clear that the affair had not ended. In one very painful session, Bill was able to admit to Kathy that he was very confused, that he felt drawn to Jeannette, but that he really wasn't sure he wanted out of the marriage. He also admitted that things had gone much further with Jeanette than he had originally admitted. The truth was that they were having sex, and that he couldn't bring himself to end the relationship. What he wanted, he said, was time. As much as it hurt Kathy to hear Bill confirm that he was still involved with Jeannette, she expressed some relief, because she felt, finally, that he was being truthful. She told him that, strange as it seemed, she felt safer with him now that things were out in the open. Bill was then able to tell her how ashamed he was for being such a liar, and that he could understand how badly his lies had hurt her.

It's important to understand that admission is a painful act for both the discoverer and the discovered. In this instance, you'll notice, admission did not mean that Bill had stopped his affair, nor did remorse mean that he was ready to. What it did mean was that Kathy now knew, for the first time in many months, how Bill was feeling and what had really happened. She was, of course, hurt and angry, but she was also relieved to know the truth, and, even more important, that Bill was now being honest with her. Although Kathy didn't hear what she wanted to, and Bill found it so hard to express his real feelings, both were later able to acknowledge that this was a turning point. It led them to a more open level of communication. It was an enormous relief to Kathy to know that she wasn't crazy, and that her suspicions had been justified. It was also a relief to Bill to be able to talk about the secret that he had carried for such a long time. It felt good not to have to lie anymore. Still, he wasn't sure that he could sever the relationship with Jeannette, and he wasn't yet ready to tell Kathy that.

The Truth Doesn't Come Out All at Once

Admitting the truth and expressing remorse are a beginning, but it would be optimistic to assume that, simply because the door to honesty has been opened, it will stay open. The discoverer will continue to want details, corroboration of suspicions, dates and times. Patience and perseverance are required of both partners. Remember also that there are different types of infidelity. Each carries with it its own problems:

If the Involved Partner Is Having an Affair

Involved partners may still be confused, even though they have admitted the affair and shown remorse about the lying. Because of this confusion, they may promise that they will stop seeing the other person but sometimes can't bring themselves to. The best possible case is that they will admit their confusion, and stop hiding what they're doing. The worst case, of course, is that the lying will continue. The wise mate will do everything possible to make it clear to the involved partner that it is the truth that's most needed.

If the discoverer hopes that the marriage will survive, he or she should know that confusion, as opposed to certainty, is a good sign. When they are confused, people tend to keep talking with their mates. This often brings them closer together, even though the talk is very stressful. Many couples report that recovery wasn't a "one-shot miracle," but instead a series of events, many painful conversations and revelations. In these conversations, they can talk carefully and honestly about the confusion. If the couple can keep things out in the open this way, it's better. Affairs thrive in the dark. Many people report that the affair looks less enticing as the couple talks honestly. Another virtue of good talk is that the couple begins to be a "we" again, two of us facing a problem together.

This does not mean that the problem is over. The involved partner has also formed an attachment to the affair partner, so it shouldn't be surprising that it may take time before the relationship is completely severed. Remember, the third party often believes that soon the marriage will end, and that the involved partner will now be free to marry him or her. Given this, the involved partner may feel a strong need to meet a number of times with the third party in order to deal with that person's pain and anger.

The third party may also threaten to wreck the marriage by calling and revealing still more details about the affair. This only serves to increase the shame, guilt, and anxiety that so many unfaithful partners are already experiencing. They know that they have hurt both their mate and the third person. They feel split down the middle as they try to repair the damage that they have done. Many experience the agony of knowing that whatever they now do, one of the two will be badly hurt.

As the involved person struggles to clean up the mess, his or her partner often feels (and maybe rightly so, at least at first) that the mate's worry is more about hurting the third party than about hurting the noninvolved partner. If the involved person picks up on this, he or she will work to cover their tracks better as they continue contact with the affair partner whom they are now trying to dump or are still ambivalently involved with. Many discoverers feel hopeless at this point, thinking, "This is just more of the same lying and cheating—I give up." However, this kind of behavior is really often an indication that the affair is dying. Another sign of the affair's death is a series of phone calls, hang-ups, or, in extreme cases, stalking. All of these actions indicate that the third party is feeling hurt and abandoned.

The probability that ambivalent partners will decide that they want to remain in the marriage is relatively high. Of course, there are some whose ambivalence is leading them to the conclusion that the marriage must end. We'll look at some of the issues that come when one member makes this decision in the next section. For now, we'll continue to explore the restoring of trust.

If the Involved Partner Is a Philanderer

The wives of many Don Juans believe at first that the addictive behavior is merely flirtatious. At a certain point, they begin to face the painful truth. Too many details have piled up, too many questions left unanswered. It is then that the addict's wife is overcome not only with how much she doesn't know about this man but also with the fear that she may have contracted a disease from him because of his irresponsible behavior. Chances are that her initial attempts at confrontation will be met with absolute denial. It may take many tries before the mask comes off. Remember that his addictive behavior has been his attempt to fight his fear of abandonment.

Most sexual addicts don't want their marriages to end. To the extent that you want to continue the marriage, this gives you a certain power. Fred's story provides a good example.

The first time I heard Fred speak on the telephone, he spoke so softly and hesitantly that I could barely make him out. He told me that his wife, Belle, had given him my number, and that he needed to see me right away because he was in deep trouble. An appointment was made, and the next day I met him. He was about forty-five years old, handsome and well-dressed. He was the president of a large manufacturing firm, with its factory in another state. He generally spent a day a week at his apartment near the factory, but for the most part, traveled around the country seeking new business.

With great embarrassment, Fred told me that he had never gone to any city without trying to find what he called "some chippy" to spend the night with. "I don't know why I do it," he said, "but I feel like I must do it. It's really nuts, because there couldn't be a better bed partner than Belle—or a better wife. You must help me—she's kicked me out. I don't know if I can live without her." The more we talked, the more tumbled out. He told me he couldn't believe what he was telling me. For years he had hidden his acts from everyone. He was a pillar of his community. He was his kids' soccer coach. If this got out, he could never again face his community, his kids, or his employees. He explained that he had been doing this since he was about seventeen years old, which was also just about the time he met Belle.

Belle called me after Fred's session and told me that she really loved him, but that he would never again set foot in their home until he had truly faced himself and the enormity of the pain he had caused her. She agreed to come to one session, but only to lay out her demands, not to be part of the therapy. "This is Fred's problem," she insisted, "and he's got to do this by and for himself." Fred pleaded for just one more chance, but Belle responded, "I couldn't possibly believe you right now. I love you, but I can't even stand the sight of you. Fix yourself up, understand why you do this. Then we'll see." In the end, they made the following deal. Fred would stay at his plant and not come home at all until they both agreed he was ready. Fred would come in every Thursday, take a hotel room, and attend therapy three times before going back. The only place he would see her, she informed him, would be in therapy but only when he was in control of himself.

In the end, Fred agreed. In therapy, he expressed enormous relief that he could at last talk to someone about what he had been doing. He knew that if he could only stop his womanizing now, he stood a chance with Belle.

Even though his insight was growing, he still had an occasional slip while on one of his trips. He was able to find a chapter of Sex Addicts Anonymous where he was comforted to know that he was not alone in having this problem and where he gained still more understanding about his addiction and its control. One day he called Belle to let her know that he had just celebrated half a year of abstinence from addictive sex. He asked her if she would go out for dinner with him to celebrate this important milestone. She did, and it wasn't long before they got back together. It was the first time in his life that he experienced a faithful marriage. In their last meeting with me, Belle said, "As important as it is to me that I can now trust Fred, I think it means even more to him, because now he can trust himself."

The fact that Belle took such a strong stand was an important turning point for Fred. Although his dependence on her (this is very typical of sexual addicts) was in itself unhealthy, it acted to their advantage as a couple. It was urgent to Fred that he not lose Belle, so her declaration that she loved him but would not accept him until he faced his problem triggered his willingness to enter therapy wholeheartedly. This is not always the case, as we will see in a later section of this chapter.

If the Involved Partner Had a One-Night Stand

It is important to differentiate between a one-night stand and compulsive anonymous sex. If it comes to light that a person has *frequent* one-night stands during the course of an exclusive relationship, they are not considered to be true one-nights stands. It's a safe bet that the person who has many one nighters is sexually addicted, and that the mate is only seeing the tip of the iceberg.

Here, however, we will limit ourselves to discussing true one-night stands.

Like other forms of infidelity, a one-night stand can occur in any exclusive relationship. One-nights stands can be the result of curiosity, boredom, a few extra drinks at a convention, or even social custom.

George and Martha were both in their mid twenties. They had been married for less than a year, but she was ready to divorce him. They had been going together for several years before they married and were faithful to each other during their courtship. Each knew that the other had relationships with several people in the years before they began their courtship. Neither was upset about this.

What devastated Martha was what happened at George's bachelor party. The party had been held at a private club. Her brother, who was a guest at the party, reported to her that, during the course of the party, George had gone off, at the urging of his friends, to have sex with one of the "dancers," who was a prostiute they had hired for the evening. A day or two before the wedding, Martha had questioned George intensely and angrily. George said that the girl had danced for him, and he had put money in her waistband, but he absolutely denied that he'd had sex with her. Martha accepted this, although she found it disgusting.

During the months following the marriage, more and more stories came to Martha's attention. Now she was positive that he had indeed had sex with the young woman. She was furious. He'd had sex—that was wrong—and he had lied to her about it. That was even more wrong. She confronted him again, and after a stormy couple of hours, he sheepishly admitted it. Thinking that she would now be relieved, hearing the truth at last, George was unprepared for her rage.

"Boys will be boys," he insisted. "It's just a guy thing. The other guys goaded me on—I couldn't not do it." The more he tried to justify it, the angrier she became. Now Martha's focus shifted. "Look at all the excuses your making. The fact is, I asked you a million times, and you lied a million times. Now you expect me to believe you? And how impressionable are you? Do I have to think that every time you're out of my sight, if somebody goads you on, you'll do something?"

As the dust cleared, George and Martha were able to see that, beyond the issue of the lying about the sex, there was a deeper problem. George always wanted to be the good guy, to please people and never hurt anyone's feelings. This often led him to tell lies. These lies tended to get him in deeper and deeper trouble. In the end, Martha assured George that the most important gift he could give her was honesty. She couldn't bear the thought of a lifetime of being his policeman. They even made a deal. George promised that the next time he was tempted to tell a "coverup" story, he would instead tell the truth. Martha promised George that, no matter what the truth was, she wouldn't get wild about it, but they would talk until they came to some agreement about it.

It wasn't long before they had a chance to test their new agreement. George approached Martha carefully. "I want to be straight with you. I was tempted to just tell you that I have to go to a bachelor party for my friend, but the truth is, I know that there will be prostitutes there. The thing is, he came to my party, and I would really hurt his feelings if I didn't go to his." Martha described her fears but tried to keep calm as she did it. George listened carefully. He told her that he really understood how she felt now, and because he could feel for her worries, he knew that he would have the strength not to get involved. When he came back from the party, she was waiting for him. They talked about what had happened, and he could honestly tell her that he had not participated, although he knew that things that were distasteful to her had happened.

This was the beginning of a significant change in their relationship. They learned early in their marriage that they would not always see eye to eye, but if they spoke honestly, they could still respect each other. They also agreed that their own concept of monogamy was that sex was a private act, reserved for the two of them.

If George and Martha's fight had stayed only on the topic of the party and what he did there, nothing would have been gained, and she might have decided to go through with the divorce that she thought she wanted. What they did instead was work together, as hard as it was, to change the way they talked about difficult subjects. Several years later, they both agreed that, since the stag party, they had experienced several problems with an honesty that they had never before achieved. Both agreed that the crisis about the stag party was a turning point in their marriage.

When Trust Can't Be Restored

While a commitment to be truthful doesn't guarantee that a relationship will continue, it does set the stage for either a better relationship or a better ending. Choosing to live with untruthfulness, however, condemns couples to living out their days in a mutually hurtful, emotionally deadening environment.

Betty had been married for over twenty-five years to Philip, a quiet, inward man, who never had shown much affection. It began to dawn on her one day that he was showing a remarkable interest in his secretary. He began to get up about an hour early each morning, claiming that his secretary's car was broken, and that he was picking her up to take her to work. Betty also noticed that, although he generally hated to answer the telephone, now he rushed to pick it up. She thought she heard him call someone "sweetheart" when he picked up the phone one day. He hadn't called her sweetheart in years. She became obsessed with what she now thought of as Philip's affair but never seemed to get enough proof to convince herself. She couldn't trust her intuition, she said. She had also asked him many times, and he had told her that she was crazy. Eventually she consulted a private detective, asking him to check up on Phil's activities. He reported that each morning Phil got to his secretary's door about an hour before work and came out with her about an hour later. He brought her back at about five o'clock, and stayed till about six. "But that doesn't prove anything," she told the investigator, who then asked her to tape Philip's telephone conversations. When she listened to them, she could never be sure exactly what they meant except that she kept hearing endearing words. Again she asked and again Philip denied. Eventually the investigator quit the case. His final words to Betty were, "Lady, you just don't want to know." This helped Betty see that she had made her choice—that whatever happened, she was staying in the marriage. She was too afraid of all the changes she would face.

For many people however, one member of the couple—sometimes both—reach a point where they can no longer bear the dishonesty and the deadness. At this point, all of the long-stored hurt and rage can finally erupt. This can set the stage for a final and miserable ending. When people have not talked out what went wrong and mourned the death of their relationship, the hidden hurts leave bitterness that may be manifested by one person refusing to let go, causing fury in the other. It can lead to bitter and sometimes endless litigation, often to the point that estates are destroyed. In these bitter divorces, not only husband and wife but also children suffer. I strongly recommend that, if a couple is moving towards a bitter divorce, they seek counseling with a qualified family therapist to try to create a better environment for negotiating a decent divorce.

Clear Signs

There are some signs that mean that a point of no return has been reached. The clearest is, of course, the absolute refusal to admit an infidelity despite powerful evidence that it is ongoing.

The second is the absence of any expression of remorse for the pain that lying has caused.

The third is that sometimes even truth and remorse can't revive love.

Remember

- Reestablishing trust can be a long and difficult process

- There may be setbacks along the way

- Admission and remorse are crucial, even if the relationship doesn't continue

- Establishing trust is worth the effort—it will give you a better marriage or a better divorce

Surviving
Infidelity

The previous chapter dealt with the struggle to regain trust. In this chapter you'll see some situations in which couples achieve new levels of trust, honesty, and communication, and others in which the involved mate can't bring him or herself to a higher level of honesty so that the deceit continues. I'll also detail situations in which, even though there has been admission and remorse, the discoverer simply can't accept what she or he has learned and must leave the relationship.

Whether the relationship survives or dies, certainly each individual has a right to a healthy life beyond the infidelity. I'll discuss situations in which the couple benefits from the discovery of an affair. Then I'll talk about the effects of other types of infidelity. Last, I'll illustrate cases in which one person must face alone the issues that the infidelity has uncovered, because the other refuses to.

Affairs: The Phases of Recovery

I'd like to present the phases of recovery following an affair's discovery as if they occurred in some orderly progression, each step coming in its place. It would be wonderful if things worked this neatly, but they seldom do. So, as you read, it will be important to remember that issues from one phase will tend to come up again, even if you think they've been settled and left behind. With that warning in mind, here are the phases of recovery.

Phase One: Restoring Trust

The loss of trust hurts so much that it keeps the discoverer constantly on guard against the possibility of further betrayal. When the involved mate can unequivocally admit that the infidelity occurred, the partner almost invariably feels a sense of relief. For months, maybe even years, the person has been told that he or she is crazy to think something was going on. Now, at last, they know that they were quite sane.

During the time that they were being given false information, most people start looking as if they were crazy. In chapter 3, I characterize this phenomenon as "cold rage." During this time, the partner's behavior becomes erratic. They're irritated at the slightest thing—and have no idea why. Just under the surface, an awareness is slowly growing that a terrible thing is happening—but they feel forced to bury their feelings because of the false reassurance they're getting. Both discoverers and those discovered agree that the term "cold rage" beautifully describes the irritability and doubt the discoverer experiences before the affair is revealed. Many involved partners also report that the apparent "craziness" of their mate made them feel all the more justified in their affairs—after all, who would want to stay at home to be with such a crazy, unpredictable person?

Honesty Produces Trust

The normal reaction to trauma is to be on your guard. A period of increased trust often comes to an abrupt halt if some bit of evidence, some lie that is not yet explained, comes to light. Sometimes this happens purely by accident. A wife is going over the phone bills, as she has for years, but this time she notices that, a few months ago when her husband told her he was in Idaho at a business meeting and couldn't be reached, he had placed calls to her from Honolulu! Her thoughts flash back to that time. She had begged him just to tell her the truth. He swore to her that nothing was happening, and that he was dying to get back from his boring meeting. But he was lolling on the beach with this other person.

Her immediate impulse was to let her anger work itself up, and then confront her husband with this new bit of evidence. Instead, she decided to have a good talk with herself first. It went something like this:

- This is old news.

- I know he had an affair—he's already admitted it.

- This reminds me that he *was* unfaithful, but it doesn't mean he's still cheating on me.

- I feel I need to share this with him. I'm afraid that if I don't, my hurt and anger will only come out in a bad way at some later time.

- I need to let him know that the more lies he can reveal to me before I discover them, the safer I'll feel. That way I'll be in for fewer surprises.

- I think I'm ready to talk about it in a calm way now.

When she approached her husband, he also needed to prepare himself for this difficult conversation. He began his own self-talk:

- I am going to put myself in her shoes. I know she's been badly hurt, and my lying was what hurt her.

- If I were in her shoes, I could see this as a powerful reminder to keep her guard up—that maybe I'm still involved.

- I know my tendency is to get nasty and defensive when she makes one of these discoveries.

- I have to find the words to let her know that I understand how hard it must be for her when old reminders turn up.

- I am going to be absolutely up front. Any questions she asks, I will answer as accurately as I can.

Because each of them had done the necessary homework, they were able to get through this difficult encounter feeling that they had made some more progress. Both were willing to be absolutely honest. It is this honesty that is at the heart of a good marriage. *Honesty is the necessary prelude to trust. Trust is the prelude to intimacy.*

Sometimes the process of regaining trust doesn't proceed so easily. This is particularly true if the involved mate has further contact with the third party (in the case of an affair) or continues other types of unfaithful behavior, such as sexual addictions. These issues will be discussed later in this chapter.

In order to examine some of the twisty paths that bring a couple toward trust, let's return briefly to the case of Bill and Kathy, which was discussed in the last chapter. One night, after several good weeks, Bill came home many hours late. Kathy was worried and anxious. Bill explained that he had seen Jeannette, but only to tell her that he could no longer go on with both relationships and wanted to give his marriage a chance. Kathy wanted very much to believe what he was saying but had a rush of emotions. She was hurt that he still had contact with Jeannette, angry that he was late without telling her, and not at all sure that she could believe that his meeting with Jeannette was, as he claimed, an attempt to refocus himself on the marriage.

Kathy confided in a friend about this latest development. The friend was extremely sympathetic to her but told her that she thought Kathy was a fool to ever trust Bill again. Later, when things were better, Kathy resented her friend for offering her advice so freely. It made her feel even more angry and suspicious.

It took Bill and Kathy many weeks to return to a higher level of trust. During this time, Kathy required constant reassurance. Bill offered this in the form of increased phone calls to her during the day, letting her know where he was at all times, and showing her much more affection and attention. At the same time, he was able to tell her that he was sad that he had hurt Jeannette, and was sometimes depressed not only because he didn't like the way he had acted toward both of them, but also because he missed the high that he had felt during the affair.

The high that Bill describes is comparable to the high that people experience with drugs or alcohol. Highs are unnatural but very desirable states. After the high, people begin to experience a down feeling and often regret their addictive behavior. However, since the high feels so good, they may go back to the addictive behavior in order to relieve the down feeling. Because of its addictive nature, people involved in an affair often experience this same ambivalence. They want the affair to continue, but may at the same time feel that there is really something unhealthy about it. Because of this, time may be on the side of the marriage. In the down phase, the affair-involved person often feels once again pulled toward the marriage.

The Affair Bubble

In chapter 3 I described how affairs begin, and particularly how they are often just drifted into. Many people experience their affair as a kind of private bubble. Once the bubble bursts, many couples are prepared to talk honestly. Couples often report that they have never talked as much or as deeply with one another as they do during the phase of rebuilding trust. The effort put in during this period has the additional advantage of bearing dividends later. The honesty and trust that is being developed can now be applied not only to talking about the affair and its aftermath, but about the marriage itself. When this turning point occurs, it paves the way for the second phase of recovery—the marriage review.

Phase Two: Reviewing the Marriage

Regaining trust and putting the infidelity aside are not sufficient to move a couple toward a better marriage. The marriage review is a process that helps both partners to develop a new set of skills that will enable them not simply to withstand the crisis but to find in it the seeds of a stronger relationship. To begin this review, it's necessary to make a serious commitment of time. After all, the future of your marriage may well depend on this effort. For some couples, once or twice a week is sufficient. Others require daily talks until they get beyond the estrangement that is part of the affair's aftermath. Even if something comes up that you feel requires urgent attention, try hard to hold it off until the time you've agreed on. Use your journal to write about what you need to talk about. Then when you do get to talk, you will feel more organized and clear-headed. Make sure that the time chosen insures that there will be no interruptions. If you have one, put on your telephone answering machine. Put away your beepers. You will also need to set aside some time to think alone about what you are learning as you talk together. Your journal can be a big help in using your alone time well.

First Things First

Once you have decided on a time and a place, set some ground rules about how to speak with one another. The purpose of setting rules is to assure that the conversations will help you to break new ground, rather than endlessly repeating old issues. The most important skill is to begin to listen well and to become deeply aware of your partner's feelings. Techniques that promote empathic listening—listening with the heart—were described in chapter 5. Be sure to use these skills as you speak together. People don't change because someone begs them to or orders them to. They don't make successful deals about change, either. Deep change comes when you can truly feel what your partner is feeling. If you care for your partner, and you become aware of a deep hurt you have caused, you *want* to change it. Here are some ground rules:

In any given conversation, let one person do most of the talking. This can be done in terms of who has something urgent to talk about, or by tossing a coin. The listener's job is to draw out the talker. This is not as easy as it seems. Avoid leading questions. They make a conversation seem more like a courtroom. The only purpose of the question is for the listener to be drawn deeper into what the talker is saying. Here are a few reminders that insure sensitive listening.

- Listen attentively to the content of what is being said.

- Listen attentively for the feelings that may underlie the content.

- Look directly at the person.

- Be aware of what your body is saying. If you shake your head "no," your partner will feel it and shut down or become defensive.

- Draw your partner out as completely as possible, losing yourself in his or her feelings.

- Struggle not to answer what is being said. Your job is to hear, not respond.

- Avoid comparing your feelings to the other person's. If he says, "I have felt so burdened by work, and I never felt that you cared," be careful not to say, "Me too."

- Stop after a few minutes to paraphrase the other, and if possible, to describe in your own words what you think the person might be feeling.

The talker must work to find words that are not inflammatory. If you are highly charged emotionally or if you yell, scream, or cry, you are likely to raise the listener's defenses, which stops good empathic listening. So don't emote, but instead find words to describe what you're feeling. Speak in "I" language, not "you" language. "I feel worried and neglected when you're going to be late and don't call," as opposed to, "You never call, you make me furious—you're a disgusting, uncaring pig." Remember, you're trying to get your mate to feel what you feel, not humiliate him or her.

Couples also make up their own rules for good talk, based on their greatest fears about each other. One couple designed a very brief contract: He wrote: "I promise that I will not say 'I don't know' when you ask me what I feel. I'll try to put it into clear words." She wrote: "I promise not to shout and scream, no matter how upset I am."

What to Talk About

Many people begin by talking about their courtship and early marriage. It's good to remember how you met, what attracted you to each other, and good experiences that you shared early on. By the time an affair has occurred, many couples have forgotten what it was that drew them together and how pleasant many of their early experiences were. Couples report that this kind of conversation has great emotional impact. It's also important to talk about troubles the couple experienced early in the marriage. Although he had been married for over thirty years, one man had never before spoken about his hurt that his then young wife called making love "my wifely duty." This led to an important conversation about her strict upbringing and its impact on her feelings about sexuality. Although neither felt that the conversation led to any new ideas, they were surprised to discover that, following it, their love life improved enormously. In this instance, it wasn't logic that caused change—it was the remarkable power of empathy.

Conflict Resolution

A major cause of affairs is the failure of a couple to learn good ways to solve problems. Often the inability to talk honestly about feelings and thoughts that might be considered shameful or embarrassing makes it almost impossible to talk about problems. If they stay underground, they can't be resolved. As one woman put it, "If I couldn't tell him that it upset me that he came to bed without washing up, how was I ever going to find a way of telling him I was losing my love for him and had gotten involved with someone else?" People have found all sorts of ways to avoid dealing with important issues. Here are two that have been described by the family therapist Lyman Wynne (1958):

Pseudohostility is the use of continual bickering and turmoil to help keep a relationship together. It may seem a strange idea, but some couples are so uncomfortable with deep feelings that they stumble on strange solutions. This is how pseudohostile couples have learned to stay together. They express all feelings through fights about things that are so unimportant that later it's impossible even to remember what they were about. As long as couples maintain their pseudohostile behavior, they never can even begin to talk about the things that truly bother them the most. So, of course, nothing can change, and no problems can be solved.

Pseudomutuality is still another way in which families avoid intimacy. Pseudomutual families go to remarkable lengths to avoid conflict. On the surface everything seems cheerful and smooth. Such families seem like those wonderful family TV shows of the fifties, but under the surface, important issues are constantly avoided. As with pseudohostility, the end result is the inability to solve problems.

As you look at your own relationship, ask yourselves if your communication seems like pseudomutuality or pseudohostility. Can you see other ways in which you have constructed your relationship that keep you from talking clearly with each other? You may find it very hard to talk about these patterns with each other at first. After all, if you've had a history of difficulty in communicating, it stands to reason that it would be hard to talk now about the very act of communication itself. So this is a good time for each of you first to do some private preparation. Take out your journals and each begin to write about things that you wish you had been able to talk about in the past, but feel you have never been successful with. Keep your list of topics for later—don't try to bring them up just yet. Instead, write down what you think has prevented successful talk about these issues until now. One man's log looked like this:

Things That Bother Me

- She always seems more interested in the kids than in me.

- She seems so disappointed in my career—it makes me feel as if she doesn't really respect me as a man.

- She spends money in crazy ways— I'm always afraid we'll go under.

How Do I Communicate about Things?

- About the kids—I keep my mouth shut, but I boil inside. Maybe that's why I just disappear into the TV.

- About the money—I shout and scream—and I make fun of her. I guess I can be very sarcastic.

- About my career—I keep my mouth shut, for the most part. But when she talks about how great other guys are doing, I'll probably end up picking a fight about something entirely different later that day.

His wife wrote:

Things That Bother Me

- The only time he ever shows any affection is when he wants sex. I hate that—and then, when we get into bed, the last thing I want to do is have sex. I can't understand—when we were younger, it was so good together.

- He's so crude with the kids—he makes fun of them and puts them down all the time. Sometimes I feel like I've just stayed in the marriage to try to protect them from his sarcasm. Come to think of it, it's the same way he talks to me a lot of the time. I wish I could get him to change.

- All he ever seems to think about is his job, how much he hates it, how tired it makes him.

How I Communicate

- About sex—I do anything I can to avoid it. When I do it, I kind of submit, but in a way that has to make him mad to know that that's all I'm doing. I'm not really there—just my body.

- About the kids—I don't say anything much to him, but behind his back, I side with them. I know it makes him angry, but because I do it behind his back, we never really talk about it.

- About his job—I make fun of his being tired all the time. But really, I'm so angry because he seems more devoted to it than to me.

Changing the Rules of Communication

As you go through your own journal loggings, focus at first away from the content—sex, the kids, work, etc.—and stay on the subject of how you are communicating with each other. Share the communication section of your journal with each other. As you talk, be sure that you are dealing only with what you'd like to change in the way *you* communicate, and not the changes you would like to see in your partner. Resist the temptation to tell your partner how you want him or her to change. If you can do this successfully, you will begin to see that each of you is taking personal responsibility for your own role. Then you will begin to notice that a "we" position is beginning to develop. Remember—the moment you attack the other person, the feeling of "we" dissolves, and you will each then become defensive. Because of the defensiveness, you'll most likely revert to your old and unsuccessful ways of communicating. As an example of how a "we" position develops, here are some of the conclusions of the couple described above:

- We bury a lot of things. Instead of really talking about them, we seem to almost pretend that they don't exist—but it doesn't mean we aren't bothered about them.

- We really use sarcasm a lot—and we both seem to do it. If things are going to change, we'll really have to be aware of that. We'll each have to take personal responsibility for curbing the sarcasm.

- We communicate a lot more by what we don't say than by what we do. We agree that we both avoid sex as a way of saying we're disappointed or angry.

Once you have agreed on how you'll communicate, you're ready to begin talking about your marriage itself. As you do this, try hard to avoid talking about the infidelity, and stick to the topic of your own relationship. However, if the discoverer has renewed suspicions, or is having flashbacks or other signs of a post-traumatic reaction, it's urgent that the involved partner be extremely supportive and attentive. With this reassurance, it is usually possible to proceed with the marriage review. Remember, don't try to crowd too much into a single meeting together. Give yourselves time to journal and think about the new ideas that your conversation is raising.

When Did Things Begin to Go Wrong?

Once you have developed some ground rules, one useful way of reviewing your marriage is to pinpoint when things began to change. Try the following. Make two pieces of paper that look like this:

Low		High
1	5	10

Each of you should then list the years of your courtship, and then of the marriage itself, down the left margin of the page. Next to it, put your rating for each year. You may have no clear idea why you've rated a certain year with a certain number—don't worry about it. Just let your feelings guide you. After you've both done this, notice how close your evaluations are, or how far apart. You will probably notice that there is a good degree of agreement about when things began to go wrong.

If, as is often the case, the courtship and early years get relatively high ratings, talk about what was good then, what you miss and hope you might restore. Such talk can help you to see what your strengths as a couple have been. Don't be surprised if this conversation leaves you feeling much closer to one another. When couples do this particular exercise, they often tell me that they had all but forgotten what attracted them to each other, and what they loved about one another. They feel closer as they reminisce. From this perspective, it is a little easier to begin to face and try to understand what happened when, in a certain year of the marriage, the rating went down.

As you come to the first really low-rated year, each of you should make your own list of what was going wrong that year. As an example, here is one couple's evaluation. Donald wrote:

Fifth Year

• Began to feel pushed away (by wife).

- First time I thought about whether getting married had been a wise choice.

- Sex, which had been really good, was going down in quality and quantity.

Grace wrote:

Fourth Year

- After the stillbirth of our first baby, I felt dead inside. I just couldn't get beyond my grief.

- I really didn't want anyone near me—I don't know why.

- Donald's attempts to get me involved in sex seemed so crass to me. Why was he bothering me if he knew I didn't want it? Why didn't he give me more comfort?

You'll notice a difference of a year in their estimates of when things began to slide downward. This is not unusual. People don't always see things in exactly the same way. So they began to look at why the time around their fourth and fifth year of marriage was so strained. As they shared their lists with each other, they decided to write down all the things that had happened in that span of time. Here is their list:

Fourth and Fifth Year

- My father (Grace's), with whom I was very close, died in an automobile accident. He was about fifty-five years old, and in excellent health. He'd been jogging when he was killed.

- I (Donald) got a big promotion at work, which entailed a lot of long distance traveling.

- We moved from the city into the suburbs.

- I (Grace) felt very isolated. The fact that I didn't drive made me very dependent on other people, and it made you (Donald) angry that I didn't want to learn. I felt that I was dragged out here, and that I was living your dream. We didn't even really discuss it. I felt like I was kidnapped!

Using your own journal entries, talk now about what you agree was your first difficult year. Work hard to listen empathtically—if you can enter into each others' feelings, you are listening with the heart. This couple realized that they had barely discussed the many stresses that were going on at once. Each felt that they were isolated, going it alone. What can you agree on about difficult times in your marriage?

Protecting the Affair Partner

Grace and Donald were making good headway. They were talking now about their marriage, not the affair. They were beginning to see old, negative patterns in which they had both participated. Because they could now see these patterns so clearly they had stopped blaming each other. This progress strengthened their belief that they had negotiated the trust phase well in the six months since the affair.

It was just at this point that telephone hang-ups, which had become a regular part of Grace's life, became much more frequent. She told Donald that she knew they were coming from his affair partner. He neither agreed nor disagreed. Grace wasn't comfortable with his response but couldn't put her finger on why it bothered her so much.

One day the calls took a new turn. Grace began getting calls from people whom she couldn't identify by voice at all. Sometimes they were men, sometimes women. The things they were saying were horrible. They told her new details of Donald's affair—things he'd never told her. They told her that there had been other affairs. Sometimes they told her that he was still seeing Frances. She tried hard to understand what was happening. One thing she noticed was that Donald never got the calls—only the hang-ups. Only she got both the calls and some hang-ups. When she did get calls, she couldn't identify them with her Caller ID—they were all from blocked numbers. She felt very confused and frightened, and turned to Donald for help and reassurance.

When she described to Donald what she'd observed, he told her at first that he'd be comfortable trying to go through all of the accusations and help to identify those that were true—old details that he hadn't yet talked about with Grace, maybe even forgotten—and those that weren't. He assured her that one of the things that most certainly wasn't true was that the affair was still going on.

In one of these conversations, Grace mentioned that it seemed still clearer to her that these calls were somehow the handiwork of Frances. "No," Donald responded, in a tone that Grace didn't like at all. "She's not that kind of person. She'd never do something like that." Now Grace was furious. "You're putting her ahead of me. How dare you. If you think so much of her, why don't you get the hell out of here and go off with her?"

Now Donald was equally angry. "Why do we have to talk about Frances? She's not the issue. The issue is us, our marriage. I want the marriage, but you're letting these stupid calls bring us down."

Romanticizing the Affair Partner

Donald's response to Grace's accusation about Frances's connection to the phone calls was not unusual. Because affairs occur in a bubble, it's hard for the involved partner to see the affair partner's imperfections. Donald remembered the good and carefree times with Frances. It was hard for him to even imagine her doing something so vengeful—nor did he want to. A piece of him still wanted to keep his memories of the affair in a little compartment of his mind, a kind of a drawer in which to store them—a private place, just for himself. He found it difficult to understand why it was so upsetting for Grace that he wasn't able to grant that Frances was responsible for the calls. It was only when he began to get calls at his office from Frances herself that he realized how angry Frances was with him. Now he heard, directly from Frances, the threat that if she couldn't have him back, she would do everything in her power to poison his marriage.

It was only then that he was able to realize why Grace was so angry when he had denied that Frances was behind the calls. When he explained this to Grace, she seemed a little relieved, but still very distant.

Holding On to Suspicion

It took Grace well over a month to put this new crisis into perspective. She bitterly resented what she saw as his loyalty to Frances. Worse, it reminded her of all of her old suspicions. One day she found herself mindlessly reviewing a stack of old telephone bills, looking once again for more clues. It frightened her that she was still searching. After all, Donald seemed so attentive and involved in the marriage. They had continued their agreed-upon conversations about the marriage itself, and they were going well. So why couldn't she just let go?

She wanted so much to get beyond her fear, but she couldn't see a way out. One day she blurted out: "Donald, I've got to let go of these suspicions—they're killing me. Checking is my last protection, but I despise doing it. But what if I'm wrong, and I still should have been suspicious? Here's what I've decided. First, I need to hear in your own words that you now understand that Frances was behind the calls, and that you can understand how much your denying it hurt me. Second, I promise you I'll try hard not to be falsely suspicious. But if it turns out that my suspicions were justified, I will begin divorce proceedings the very day I find out. That's a promise."

What Grace said was as much for her own ears as for Donald's. It gave her a sense of safety. It enabled her to suspend her distrust and return wholeheartedly to working on reviewing her marriage. Grace's experience is not unique. Many discoverers find it hard to give up their suspicions, because they provide a cushion against further pain.

Additional Issues

If you have begun to examine critical times in your marriage when things went wrong and satisfaction was low, begin to look at some of the factors that may have contributed to the crisis. Read over the various issues described in chapter 2, and see if some of them apply to your marriage. Use your journal to note how these issues relate directly to your situation.

Phase Three: A Better Marriage or a Better Divorce

If the first two phases have gone well, both partners can now begin together to consider continuing a marriage based on the principle of intimacy. An intimate relationship rests on the bedrock of honesty and trust. In an honest and trusting relationship, both partners know that there is a deep and abiding pleasure in the knowledge that their relationship constitutes a special and private place, filled with memories and experiences that are theirs alone. People in such a relationship experience a level of closeness in which there is no room for a third partner. It is this trust, honesty, and intimacy that make a marriage affair-proof. There is simply too much to be lost. There is, however, another possibility. After trust and honesty have been restored, the couple may nonetheless come to the conclusion that the marriage must end. Sometimes this is because both partners can acknowledge that the affair was simply a symptom of a marriage that had already died. Sometimes it can mean that one partner has reached an irrevocable conclusion to end the marriage, regardless of the mate's feelings.

A Word of Caution to the Involved Partner

People often feel that they have found in their affair the very things that are missing in their marriage, and that if they could only extricate themselves from their marriage, they would be able to marry the new person and "live happily ever after."

In therapy, I urge a partner who holds this belief to stop and think very carefully: *Am I ready to leave this marriage because I believe I have found something better, or am I contemplating divorce because I believe that this marriage can never, under any circumstances, be a healthy and satisfying one?*

I inform the person that most experts on marital infidelity believe that the likelihood that an affair will result in a lasting relationship is small. Estimates range between 3 and 7 per cent. Given this, basing the decision to leave your marriage on the belief that you will live happily ever after with your new-found love is probably self-deluding. If you are having an affair and contemplating ending your marriage, you should look at the very real probability that it will be several years before you find a satisfying relationship, and that it is highly unlikely that it will be with the person with whom you are currently involved. If you have children, this is also the time to consider soberly the effects of divorce on children. There is overwhelming evidence that divorce is a source of great and lasting pain for many children. For these reasons, the decision to divorce is best made on the basis of the viability of the marriage, and not on the belief that what you feel for the other person is "proof" that the marriage won't work. The truth is that for many people the excitement of the affair is often simply an indicator of a marriage that may be in trouble, but not beyond repair.

For most people, an affair occurs at a time of great vulnerability. The affair really seems to be a godsend. The involved mate seems to feel fully alive again, and believes that this new person holds the key to happiness. These are the feelings that most people have in a new relationship, especially as it begins. The name that we give to these feelings is "infatuation." The dictionary defines infatuation as "a foolishly irrational love or desire," or as "being blindly in love." It takes time to sort out whether these initial feelings will turn into the kind of love that can last a lifetime, or whether they are blind love, which will in time sour.

Acknowledging Options

In some instances, one or both partners are unable to talk about the meaning of the affair, because they are too afraid of what facing where their problem might lead. Unable to talk, they can remain locked for years in pain and sorrow. The great French author and philosopher Jean-Paul Sartre wrote a play about a man who finds himself locked in a room with two strangers. The three share in the hopelessness that derives from their growing knowledge that they will never leave this room which is, of course, a metaphor for Hell. He called his play *No Exit*. In their paralysis, some people facing the possibility of divorce also see no exit. Interestingly, the reasons that follow may be cited by men or women, the discovered or the discoverer.

- I'm afraid my children would suffer unduly.

- I'm afraid my children would never forgive me.

- What if I can't deal with the financial changes?

- I don't think my mate can survive emotionally without me.

- I don't think I can survive emotionally without my mate.

- I fear my family's response to a divorce. What if they call me a quitter?

- I don't know how I could ever get back into the dating world after all these years.

- What if there's nothing better out there?

Facing the future squarely can have remarkable results. People who can do so report that, having imagined a future beyond the marriage, they realize that they could end the marriage and survive if need be. This gives them a sense of freedom—now they know that they are not trapped but can stay or leave as they see fit. One man told me: "Once I knew that I *could* leave, I felt a burst of energy. I had choices. I could give the marriage everything I had, and that way, if I had to leave, I'd feel all right in myself about it." In this case, the man decided to stay.

A woman, once she had examined her options, decided that she was ready to leave her marriage after years of angrily tolerating what became her husband's very open affair. She said, "Once I had really examined my options carefully, my fear dissipated. What had looked impossible now seemed very possible. I realized that my family would support me. I had a good friendship network, and we had plenty of money, so I knew I'd reach a reasonable settlement. I felt so calm as I told him that I wanted out. I think it was a relief for both of us."

If you feel locked in your relationship, but also hopeless about the possibility of leaving it, use your journal to write all the reasons that keep you in this position. Fold the page in half. On the left side, list the things that keep you in a "no exit" position. On the right side, imagine the advice that you would give to a good friend in a similar position. If you can't come up with any answers that are helpful, seek professional help. Getting out of the no exit position often requires consultation. Financial questions are best dealt with by a knowledgeable accountant and often by a lawyer as well. If the emotional issues seem insurmountable, you may need to see a mental health expert, such as a psychologist, social worker, or an expert in marriage and family. Be sure that if you make an appointment with a mental health expert, you make it clear that you're not there to seek answers about whether or not to end the marriage. Rather, go to explore why you can't imagine a future outside of the marriage. One patient struggled through several months of therapy, until she had dealt with all of her fears. In the end, she decided to stay in the marriage, and the infidelity issues were resolved between her and her husband. Ironically, not long after, her husband died suddenly and unexpectedly. Later, she reported that those sessions had been very meaningful to her, because they had not only prepared her for the possibility of divorce, but also for his loss through death.

The Good Divorce

Much has been written about the negative effects of divorce on children. (For a good summary, see Wallerstein and Blakeslee, 1989.) An argument can be made that there are also good divorces, in which the rights of children are respected. In her book *The Good Divorce* (1994), the psychologist Constance Ahrons studied couples who had divorced, and how the divorces affected their and their children's subsequent lives. She defines a good divorce as ". . . one in which both the adults and children emerge at least as emotionally well as they were before the divorce." "In a good divorce," she writes, "a family with children remains a family." This means that parents continue to be responsible for the emotional, economic, and physical needs of their children. Her research shows that about 50 percent of the couples she studied ended up with amicable relationships, and that these were achieved within two to three years of the initial separation.

She reminds us that most people who divorce remarry. This means that their children become part of what she calls a *binuclear* family—meaning that it remains a family despite divorce, still with two parents. Normal, healthy, but now consisting of two nuclear families, each free to develop and to interact.

It's hard to believe if you are just now contemplating divorce, but down the road, you and your partner may well either remarry or enter long-term relationships. To the degree that a marriage ends with mutual respect and a shared understanding of how it came apart, the couple is preparing itself for an amicable divorce.

In most divorces, both parents continue to love their children and want the best for them. They come to realize that this occurs best if they can form a cooperative coparenting relationship. Many divorced parents develop excellent working relationships not only with their former mates, but also with their former mate's new husbands or wives.

What If There Are No Children?

Most divorcing couples without children will have little reason to continue their relationship. However, they have much to gain from an amicable ending to their marriage. If they leave their marriage with a clear understanding of why the affair occurred, they will do so with some new ideas about what they want in a next relationship. Many marriages become affair-ready when communication is poor and people lack problem-solving skills. If you have learned this lesson well, you are less likely to repeat the same errors next time.

It is not unusual for me to see a couple through to a divorce and then to see one or both members of the couple after their divorce as well, as they continue to sort out their feelings and, in many cases, to complete their mourning at the marriage's end. Often, the last time I see divorcing people, they tell me that they'd like to come back for a visit or two when they have become serious with a new person. It has been my pleasure to see how often they approach their next relationship having learned much from the previous one.

Other Types of Infidelity

In chapter 2, I described a number of types of infidelity that have different roots than the long-term affair. While affairs involve both sexual and emotional intimacy, there are other forms of infidelity that involve only sexual acts. Emotional closeness is the furthest thing from the mind of a person involved in this type of infidelity. While on the surface these acts appear to be sexual, it would be an oversimplification to believe that their motivation is primarily sexual. These behaviors involve pursuit, conquest, and power. They involve turning women into little more than sexual objects. The psychologist Ronald Levant, coeditor of *Men and Sex: New Psychological Perspectives* (1997), describes this cluster of behaviors as "nonrelational sex," which he defines as ". . . the tendency to experience sex as lust without any requirements for relational intimacy." Among these nonrelational acts are womanizing, repetitive infidelity, and Don Juanism. To the degree that these behaviors begin to rule a person's life, they take on an addictive quality.

These behaviors develop early, long before the marriage. People who develop such behaviors are influenced by at least three factors:

1. a societal norm that tells men that women are playthings

2. a family history in which males have provided poor models of male treatment of women

3. very low self-esteem

Like affair behavior, nonrelational sex often involves deception. If a person has a compulsive sexual addiction, he has learned to be a brilliant liar and evader. He lies to get what he wants out of women, and he lies to his wife. Since sexually addictive behavior generally predates the marriage, I am going to address each partner separately. If you believe that you are a sexually addicted person, Don Juan or Donna Juana, I would suggest that you re-read the section of chapter 2 entitled "Sexual Addiction and Don Juanism" before reading on.

Sexual Addiction

The term "sexual addiction" refers to any compulsive sexual behavior that is out of control. In this instance, we are particularly concerned with the constant need to find women (or men), seduce them, have intercourse, and abandon them. There is no time or desire for any emotional attachment. The addicted person must move on, as soon as possible, to the next "conquest."

Patrick Carnes, the author of *Out of the Shadows* (1983), is an authority on sexual addiction. He points out that it is often a family pattern. In many instances, there was sexual addiction in the previous generation, often accompanied by other addictive behavior such as gambling or drinking. (I will sometimes use the term "sexual addict," although I prefer "person with a sexual addiction," because I am uncomfortable with the effect on people of being labeled.) Carnes also reports that a very high percentage of people with sexual addictions have been sexually, emotionally, or physically abused. Almost invariably, sexual addicts report feeling that, instead of being central to their parents' lives, they felt more as if they were put on earth to serve their parents' needs. Because of this, they develop an inner emptiness that finds satisfaction in their addictive behavior, where they can safely get attention without feeling the danger that they themselves will be emotionally used, as they had been growing up (and often still are, even in full adulthood).

Here is a description of sexual addiction. As you read it, note the aspects of this description that apply to your own behavior. You will notice that some qualities seem contradictory. There are two reasons for this. First, not all addicts exhibit all of the symptoms. Second, some addicts do one thing at one time, one at another.

- It's a compulsion. It is experienced as a *must*. It isn't just a wish—it feels like a need.

- There is no emotional attachment—it's a sexual act, always with overtones of power.

- It's obsessive—the question of finding the next "score" is always on the person's mind.

- It's unstoppable—it takes more and more time, and interferes more and more with the addict's work and relationships.

- It's high-risk behavior, and the risk-taking is part of the addictive high.

- Many, although not all sex addicts, have other addictions as well.

- The addict is ashamed of his or her behavior, and therefore becomes a skilled liar.

- Many addicts boast about their "scores."

- Sexual addicts are at risk of dangerous complications, including suicide, life-threatening violence, AIDS, and other sexually transmitted diseases.

Facing the Problem

If you display many of the characteristics described here and in the section of chapter 2 which describes sexual addiction, you are sexually addicted. If that is the case, and you are still hiding your behavior from your mate, there is little hope for a change in your relationship. Unfortunately, most people who have a serious addictive problem do not face it until they hit bottom. If you listen carefully to your own anxiety you may be lucky enough to get help now, before further damage is done. Here are things that you can do to begin to face your problem:

1. Read up on sexual addiction. Carnes's book and Earle and Crowe's book (see References at the end of this book) are good sources.

2. Call your local Mental Health Association. They will be able to refer you to a Sex Addicts Anonymous Group, a Sexaholics Anonymous Group, or a similar organization. There you will meet other people with similar problems and will gain support in facing and overcoming your problem.

3. Like all addicted people, there are issues that you need to deal with that have to do with the family into which you were born (or adopted). Still other issues have to do with you, your wife (or husband), and children. Seeing a competent therapist who has experience with sexual addiction and family issues is very important.

A Word to the Addict's Mate

It is traditional in the field of addiction to refer to the addict's mate as a co-dependent, or a co-addict. I am uncomfortable with that terminology for the same reason that I am uncomfortable with the term "addict." If you are married to an addict, you are locked together with that person in a sad dance that seems never to end. There is an ever-present third party who shadows every day of your relationship—your mate's addiction and your reactions to it. Carnes notes three qualities that he believes the mates of all sexually addicted people share:

They mistake intensity for intimacy. People with sexual addictions are often high-powered, successful people, whose lives are very intense. Their mates often feel as if they live from crisis to crisis. Often their troubles are related to their sexual addiction, or some other addictive behavior such as drugs or alcohol or gambling. Their mates get caught up in this frenzied activity and mistake the intensity for intimacy.

Just as some mates get caught up in the intensity, others respond with denial. Like possums, under the threat of attack they play dead—but the energy that their denial consumes exhausts and depresses them. Still others respond with anger. In any event, the partner's every move is a reaction to the addictive behavior. According to Carnes, ". . . it fills up one's life but leaves needs unmet."

They mistake obsession for care. They are as obsessed with their mates as their mates are with pursuing their addiction. The fear of abandonment provides a powerful motive to stay centered on the addict and away from oneself. Real caring, as opposed to obsession, grows out of trust and security. One benefit of the co-addict's constant worry is that, in Carnes's words, "it guarantees a connection with the addict—even when the addict is not there." Carnes describes the case of a man whose wife left him, in the grips of her addiction. He remained obsessed with her for many years. Even though she was long since gone, his obsession kept her present in his life. The price of the obsession is that the person doesn't get on with his or her own life.

They mistake control for security. Carnes reminds us: "In all relationships, there is a risk that the other might leave." The mates of addicted people work feverishly to guarantee that there will be no abandonment. To achieve this, they strive to "change" the addict—endless labor that can never be truly accomplished.

Sometimes this effort takes the form of begging or cajoling, sometimes expressions of rage, sometimes tears. Sometimes the addict is blamed, other times excused, but never confronted in a meaningful way. Taken together, these are described as "enabling" behaviors in the addiction literature. On some level, the addict's emptiness may give the co-addict a false sense of fullness, so that the co-addict need never look inward.

Facing the Problem

It is important that you begin by answering this question for yourself: *Can I stay in this relationship without losing my dignity, and perhaps my sanity?* Perhaps you have already answered "no" to this question many times but can't imagine how to extricate yourself. Perhaps you find yourself thinking, "If we could only get beyond this, he (or she) is a truly good person, and I would then want nothing more than to stay—but if he can't—I will have to leave."

In order to ready yourself for this important step, you will have to undertake actions similar to those suggested above for the addicted partner:

1. Read up on sexual addiction. As you read, be sure to focus not only on the qualities of the addict, but particularly of the co-addict. Remember, the purpose of your reading is to change yourself—there's no one else you have the power to change.

2. Call your Mental Health Association. They will help you find a Sex Addicts Anonymous or Sexaholics Anonymous spouse's group. Attend some meetings. There you will meet other people with similar problems and gain support in facing and overcoming your problem. The most important thing you will gain from this group will be to remember once again that life doesn't have to revolve solely around your mate's problems. It will help you, as the saying goes, to "get a life."

3. Just as with your mate, there are issues that you need to deal with that have to do with the family into which you were born (or adopted). It will be important for you to find a therapist who is competent in both sexual addiction and in family issues. One possible outcome of the strategy that you are working on is that at some point, because you

have changed, your partner will be ready to accompany you to this therapist.

Many partners of addicted people have threatened to leave their marriages, some of them countless times. Unfortunately, the effect of endless threats is that they serve only to maintain the addict's sense of safety and power. After all, if you have threatened so many times but never left, or have left and returned within a day or two, you have made an idle threat.

The Power of Prediction

Wise parents learn that if they threaten their children, it will not be long before their threats are ignored. It doesn't take a child long to know that he won't really be locked in his room for a year, even though his angry parent may have threatened this. *A threat is a prediction that often doesn't come true.* If instead of threatening, we *predict*, then we can *control*. If you predict that you will do something and you then do it, you have powerful control. If you predict and then don't follow through, history will prove that what you thought was a prediction was instead a threat. If your mate sees what you are saying as a threat, it will be discounted. If your mate cares for you at all and comes to understand that what you say is what you mean, you will not be discounted.

Threats are often made when you feel under the greatest stress. "If this happens once more, I'm leaving"—but when things fall back to whatever passes for normal, you don't. Predictions must be thought through carefully and announced with assurance at the proper moment.

Bringing yourself to the point where you are willing to take the powerful step of predicting is not easy. If you have fully entered into the co-addict role, it means violating all three of the convictions that Carnes attributes to co-addicts:

Mistaking intensity for intimacy: Threatening is intense and emotional. Predicting is cool and rational—but it works.

Mistaking obsession for care: When people are obsessed, they run around in circles. They take an action one moment, only to undo it in the next. When you *care*, you are clear about what you must do and calmly execute it. Once you resolve to predict, you will feel a sense of calm come over you—and your mate will feel it too. That calmness says "I mean business."

Mistaking control for security: As the mate of an addicted person, you have been unable to accept the risk that the marriage may end. As you ready yourself to predict, you are committing yourself to taking the chance that the marriage could end, and that it might be for the best. The moment that you make that shift, you no longer spend all of your energy attempting to control your partner. Now you feel the inner security of knowing that you have a life of your own, which can only be shared with your mate if he or she takes control of his or her own life, as you are now ready to take care of yours.

If you make this shift in your own behavior, it will soon tell you whether there is any likelihood that your partner is ready to face the addiction and to begin the difficult process of change. If addicted partners are motivated to change, this is the point at which they will seek out a treatment group and get some therapy—but if your mate refuses any form of help, even though you have made a clear and unequivocal stand, then the likelihood that change will occur is very small.

A Healthy Life after Discovery

Even after infidelity has been uncovered and confronted, the aftershocks of trauma often linger. It has become something of a cliché to speak of closure following deep and abiding hurt. Many writers suggest, however, that there is never a complete ending, a neat tidying-up to conclude the sadness, loss, and hurt. It's probably more correct to say that people are *changed* following trauma. People report that, at least for a good amount of time following trauma, they experience a level of alertness to danger that they had never before imagined. Describing the aftermath of traumatic life events, Ronnie Janoff-Bulman, the author of *Shattered Assumptions: Towards a New Psychology of Trauma* (1992), describes those who have healthily survived trauma this way: "They have come face to face with reality. There is disillusionment, yet it is generally not the disillusionment of despair. Rather, it is disillusionment tempered by hope."

Up to this point we have dealt with actions that need to be taken during the crisis of discovery. Now we'll turn to practices that can forward recovery. Although there is overlap between what couples who stay together and those who split up must do, there are also some skills that are particular to each. Let's begin with some principles that are fundamental to all recovery.

Finding Meaning

Ronnie Janoff-Bulman explains that those who suffer trauma experience a loss of meaning. Following a trauma, she explains, people feel that life doesn't make sense anymore. Finding a meaning for your experience can help you come to an inner peace. Stan, whose wife had an affair, reflected on how he got beyond the trauma. "One day I was really deep into my anger. Even though she swore that she loved me, that it had all been a mistake, that she wanted nothing more than a really good marriage with me, it was all I could do to keep from hitting her. Suddenly, a realization overcame me. It struck me that she was ready to leave me because of failings that I could now see in myself. I had been cold, disinterested, bossy. I could then see that her affair was a wake-up call. It told me that I had to change, I couldn't go on simply demanding that she bow down every day and beg my forgiveness. After that, each day seemed to bring a new sense of ease and calmness for me. As I changed, I discovered that I had deep, warm feelings for her that I had neglected for years." Stan's realization gave his wife's affair a meaning: it had been a warning.

Quentin, looking back on his wife's confrontation of his sexual addiction, found first a negative and then later, a positive meaning. The first meaning he found was that his marriage was over, and that he was a hopeless addict. Although this interpretation gave meaning to her confrontation, it left him with no hope. Later, he found a far different meaning. "I am so exhausted by this addiction, and now at last, I have a reason to fight it, to learn about it and change it. Thank God that she confronted me."

Resilience and Optimism

Resilience is the capacity to recover from or to adjust easily to misfortune or change. It is the ability to bounce back. If you meet a crisis with resilience, you see it as opportunity. Lacking resilience, you see only danger. Optimism is the ability to see useful possibilities even at times of crisis.

Is optimism a given, something one is born with? And if you lack it, are you a born pessimist? No, says the psychologist Martin Seligman, who has studied depression and its treatment for well over twenty-five years. For the most part, the roots of depression lie in negative ideas we learned when we were very young. An example would be a parent telling a child, "You never do anything right—you're such a monster," or "You're such a slob," or "You'll never be any good at school." Each of these messages and others like them make children feel pessimistic about their own abilities and potential. This causes what he terms "learned incompetence." Adults can also give themselves these pessimistic messages. And when they do, they become depressed. Seligman became convinced that people can overcome depression by learning to think in an optimistic fashion.

Seligman bases his work on the principles of cognitive psychology, the study of how people think. What particularly interests him is the impact of how we think on our mood and our behavior. In his book *Learned Optimism* (1990) he presents a simple method by which people can learn to think in an optimistic, "can-do" fashion, even if they have a long history of pessimistic thinking. A major tenet of cognitive psychology is that we are in a constant internal dialogue with ourselves. If we tell ourselves negative things, we will experience negative feelings and act in negative, self-defeating ways. Unfortunately, we are often unaware of the negative beliefs that underlie our thinking—but they govern our thoughts and actions nonetheless. To help bring about the shift from pessimistic to optimistic thinking, Seligman helps people to examine, understand, and change the way they talk to themselves.

To do this, he first sensitizes people to the difference between pessimistic and optimistic thought patterns. He then helps them to develop a simple technique that helps them to change their guiding thoughts. He points out that pessimistic people see problems as permanent: "If you believe the cause of your mess is permanent—stupidity, lack of talent, ugliness—you will not act to change it." After all, if you believe that you are by nature stupid, talentless, or ugly, what can you do about it? You're stuck with it. But if you see the cause as temporary, for example, a bad mood you were in, too little effort put forth, or not taking good care of your appearance, these are all things that it is in your power to change.

To help people to produce change, Dr. Seligman uses a technique developed by another important cognitive psychologist, Albert Ellis (1975), called the "ABC technique."

- **A** stands for **Adversity**. Any seemingly negative event can be considered an adversity. This could be as simple as getting an unexpectedly low grade in school, or it could be about a significant and unwanted change in your life—losing a job, discovering infidelity.

- **B** stands for the **Beliefs** you have about your adversity. Notice that what you *think* about your adversity is what will tell you what to do about it. If your thoughts are negative, you will feel badly about your adversity and make poor decisions about what to do about it.

- **C** stands for **Consequences**, meaning how you feel and how you behave following adversity.

Adversity: A college student gets a 69 in his first test in a particular course.

Beliefs: He *thinks* "I'm a terrible student, and this only proves how stupid I am. I never do anything right."

Consequence: He *feels* disappointed, angry with himself, and discouraged. He *acts* by withdrawing from the course.

Imagine that instead he had decided to fight the thought that he was stupid. He might say something like this to himself: "I'm a reasonably intelligent person. I probably just didn't exactly understand what the professor was looking for. I guess I was taking a big leap from getting one low grade to thinking that I'm stupid. After all, I finished high school with a fine average, and got into a good college."

He would now *feel* differently. He would no longer feel so discouraged or so angry and disappointed. Now, with a clearer head, he could *act* differently as well. He might begin by checking with a few other students. He would learn that the professor is a hard marker, and that many people got considerably lower grades. He might make an appointment with the professor to see where he was unclear about the subject.

So we can see how a person's beliefs influence how he feels about his adversity, and what he does about it.

As you follow this case, it becomes evident that it isn't really the adversity that causes him to feel so badly and to make a poor choice. It's the way he sees himself. The trouble is that we are often unaware that a particular way of thinking leads us to the feelings and actions that we take when we face adversity. The ABC method helps us to become aware of thoughts that cause negative and destructive feelings, which in turn lead to self-defeating actions. Now let's apply the ABC method to Melanie, who is dealing with an infidelity.

Melanie came to me because her husband had suddenly come to her to tell her that after twenty-five years and two children, he had decided that the marriage wasn't working, and he wanted a separation. That very night, he left. She was very depressed, couldn't stop crying, and was getting almost no sleep. She told me that she felt so confused and that she couldn't stop thinking about what had happened. I asked her if she would try the ABC method. She agreed, with the following results:

- A) The adversity was, of course, that he had left.

- B) Her *thoughts* were: I can't survive without him. I've never been good at taking care of myself. I lack the skills to be a single person. I believe that the world "out there" will be a frightening and negative one, and that I won't be able to survive in it.

- C) The consequence was that she *felt* frightened. Because of this, the only *action* she could think of was to try to get him back.

Use your journal now to log some aspect of *your* current situation, using the ABC method. Now stand back a little from what you have written. One way to do this is to imagine that you are talking with a friend who has this problem and feels as you do. What would you tell her or him? Using this method, try to work on the thoughts that are making you feel pessimistic. If you can argue yourself out of those thoughts, you will notice that you are feeling a bit more optimistic. Sometimes, however, people have a great deal of difficulty talking themselves out of self-defeating patterns of thinking. For this reason, Dr. Seligman has added two more steps to the ABC process:

D stands for two different skills. We'll begin with the skill of **distraction**. There are times when you are faced with a really tough problem, you can't seem to get anywhere with it, and you just spin your wheels. There are a number of things you can do to help yourself stop thinking about a problem when you don't want to, and putting it off until you are ready to face it. One is called "thought-stopping." This can be as simple as yelling aloud "Stop!!!" when you've had enough. Of course, if you are with other people, that's not a very good way, since other people may think you're out of your mind (although when you're alone, it's a powerful tool). So some people simply carry a little three-by-five card with "Stop!!!" written in big red letters. When they can't stop obsessing, they take out the card and look at it for a moment. It has the same effect as yelling "stop." Another way is to say to yourself, "Not now," but to set a time when you will sit down when you can really work on what's bothering you. Still another is to keep your journal with you and write down these thoughts. This may get them off your chest, and then at some other time you can use the skills you are learning to fight them. The letter D also stands for **disputation**. Disputation helps you to break down the beliefs that are causing you so much trouble. For example, if you messed something up, you might have found yourself thinking, "I'm such a failure—all I do is screw things up." You can fight this thought by disputing it. For example, you might say, "Do I really fail at everything? Didn't I just recently get a promotion at work? Wasn't I proud when I got my golf score down by several points? It really isn't true to say that I'm nothing but a failure." You might also remind yourself that "I'm a failure" is a very large generalization. It's a kind of "always" statement. Everyone knows that "always" and "never" statements are generally exaggerations and examples of unclear thinking. Notice that as you go through this process of disputing the negative self-talk, it seems to lose its power over you.

E stands for **energization**. If you have successfully challenged your beliefs, you'll notice that the consequences that seemed so inevitable before now seem less awful to you. In fact, you now feel ready to take some new action, and you're feeling more hopeful about your situation. Let's return to Melanie, and see how steps D and E worked for her.

Melanie found that it was very hard for her to get her anxiety down enough to dispute the ideas that were causing her so much trouble. She decided that the first thing she needed to do was to calm herself down. To do this, she decided to use several of the suggestions for distracting herself. She found that using her three-by-five "Stop!!!" card helped her. For one thing, it made her laugh at herself a little bit and brought her some relief from all the pain and sadness she'd been feeling. She remembered an old technique she had learned for achieving relaxation through deep breathing and found that helpful as well. Probably the best thing for her, in the long run, was putting the thoughts in her journal and then promising herself that she would write about them in detail later. She even set a time—just before bed each night. She found that doing this really freed her from thinking about it all the time. Not only that, but she liked the quality of the answers that she was now beginning to give to her pessimistic thinking. Here were some of her corrections:

Concerning her poor judgment: "My judgment in many matters is good. For example, I am respected in my work. Nobody there ever accused me of having poor judgment. Another thing—I've raised three kids, and a lot of the decisions rested solely in my hands. I made good decisions, and the proof is that I have basically great kids—so my judgment can't be universally bad. As far as thinking about being single—lots of people fear divorce, but I read that about 50 percent of Americans end up divorced. You don't read about many of them jumping off high buildings because of it. I guess I would really just adjust to it, like I have to other things."

Now Melanie began to feel energized. She wasn't as sad and angry, and she didn't spend most of her time thinking about her husband anymore. Instead, she noticed that she had a greater sense of hope about the future. Most important, she took a first step. She called the local "Y," found that they had a group for people in the process of separation, and decided to join it.

When Melanie went back to check her notes on part C of her original "homework," she could see how her negative feelings at that time were leading to negative actions as well. Now, with some clear thinking, she felt more energized and optimistic. She was no longer frightened.

Use your journal now to try the full A B C D E method. Pay particular attention to how you dispute negative thinking, and how you can distract when you feel your thinking is running you in circles.

Hitting Bottom

No one method works for everyone. Some people find that cognitive work seems dry and emotionless for them. It may even make them feel disappointed in themselves. They feel so overcome with emotion when they first confront this crisis that they can't seem to extricate themselves from it, and then they feel ashamed of their inability to bounce back. Other approaches may be more successful with people experiencing this. The psychiatrist Frederic Flach describes one such approach.

Like Dr. Seligman, Dr. Flach also considers the idea of resilience, but takes a very different approach than the cognitive psychologists. In the book *Resilience: Discovering a New Strength at Times of Stress* (1988), Dr. Flach defines resilience as "the ability to cope with important, potentially dangerous turning points" in people's lives. This is a two-step process: *disruption*, by which he means "giving in to stress," and *reintegration*, putting the pieces of your world back together but into a new and stronger structure.

Dr. Flach reports that, in the late 1960s, he became aware of how many of his patients were, at least for some period of time, shattered by some major turning point in their lives. At one time, he says, he would have considered them mentally ill, but now he saw them "preparing themselves for a new and higher level of adaptation." He tells us that, under stress, we hit what he calls a *bifurcation point*, a term he borrows from physics—it means a moment of extreme change. People can respond to a bifurcation point by moving toward some new and useful change, which is what he means by a reintegration. They can also respond with some very inadequate coping behavior. Merely coping means accepting the situation as it is and settling for no change. People who do this stay in a state of anguish. They are so afraid of change that their response to the crisis is to freeze in place.

When Joan discovered that her husband of thirty years had been involved with a string of women almost from the day they had married, she fell into a deep depression (this is what Dr. Flach would call the period of disruption). After about a year in therapy, with her husband well into his next affair, she had come to accept that that was who he was, he would never change, and she could do nothing about it (this is the point of bifurcation, the crossroad). She was bitterly hurt and angry and made him pay for his behavior every day by making him the witness to her martyrdom (her solution was to hold on to the marriage as it was, to keep things the same).

This behavior left Joan stuck in her marriage, without any hope of meaningful change. Imagine if she had met this moment of change with an entirely different action. First, she would have responded with the same shock, bitterness, and suffering. But what if she then decided, "I don't have to live with a man who has lied to me for thirty years. I will try to confront him to see if he's willing at least to be honest about what he has done. I'm also going to ask for a new commitment from him to the marriage, to us. If he can't or won't, I'm going to take charge of my own life. I'm going to explore how I can get out and feel safe financially and emotionally."

Here is a paraphrase of the four laws that describe the principles of disruption and reintegration as Dr. Flach sees them:

- To learn from change, we must fall apart.

- During periods of chaos, we can't know what the future will hold.

- Each time we successfully negotiate periods of disruption and reintegration, we are better prepared to face the stresses that lie ahead.

- If a crisis in our life leads nowhere, it can leave us crippled, without the strengths we will need to face other turning points in our lives.

If you are comfortable with the cognitive work prescribed by authorities like Drs. Seligman, Beck, or Ellis, you may feel put off by the idea that we *must* fall apart in order to learn from change. Your own experience may have been that you at first reacted to the shock of discovery, but then began to use your intellectual ability to start to put your world back together.

On the other hand, if you *are* falling apart, it may be comforting for you to know that this chaotic experience is, according to Dr. Flach, a natural part of the process of change.

Naturally Resilient People

After defining resilience, Dr. Flach turns his attention to people who are resilient. He reasoned that if we know what resilient people are like, we can begin to develop qualities that encourage resilience. Resilient people don't want to stay stuck. They want to make things better. They are solution-oriented, not problem-oriented. They are independent. They trust their own judgment. This has a side benefit of enabling them to talk with others without feeling forced to accept their ideas or suggestions. They have a good network of friends, including some who are good confidants. They are open-minded. They have many interests. They have a good sense of humor. They have good insight into their own thoughts and feeling and those of others. They can communicate. They can tolerate high levels of stress. They have a philosophy of life that sees them through difficult times.

These abilities can be cultivated. Use your journal to take an inventory of how many of these qualities you already possess. You may be quite pleasantly surprised. Are you using them well? What are your weaknesses? What can you do to begin to use the skills you already possess. What new skills would serve you well now? How can you go about developing them?

Forgiving

When we forgive, we cease to feel resentment for someone who has hurt us, and we express this change in our feelings to that person. The idea of forgiveness can be frightening. For many people, it implies forgetting—as in the expression "forgive and forget." So let's begin by distinguishing forgiving from forgetting. To forget means to stop remembering—to put something out of our mind. It's hard to imagine forgetting an important turning point in one's life, perhaps impossible. More important, it's a poor idea to try to forget important events. If you have lived through the discovery of infidelity and gained something from the experience, to forget it would be to dull you, to leave you unprepared for some new crisis in your life. It's hard to imagine that you'll go through the rest of your marriage without ever again entering the doldrums, for example. One would hope that if it happens again, though, a little bell would go off, leading to the following thought: "Uh-oh, I think my partner is getting that bored, empty feeling again. That was what made him so ready for an affair. This means it's time to have a good talk with him, so that we can get back on track in our own relationship. I'd better look into myself also, to see what my role is in all this." The energy of remembering can then refuel and revitalize the marriage.

Forgiveness doesn't imply condoning either. If you reach a point where you can accept the truth of your partner's remorse following an infidelity, you may feel ready to express forgiveness. This doesn't mean that you have accepted the act itself. What you have accepted is the remorse.

It's hard to grant forgiveness when it's demanded. We described earlier how the involved person may attempt to stop the outpouring of emotion that discoverers often exhibit. Sometimes forgiveness is demanded for the same reason—to put an end to the involved mate's discomfort. When people express forgiveness before they have worked through their pain, they feel as if they have sold out to their partner, simply to remain emotionally safe. When forgiveness is given on demand, it leaves a bitter residue.

At a certain point, however, you will find, if you have weathered the infidelity, that you have begun the slow process of healing. It is then that you and your partner may be able to start the process of forgiving. This is a time to clear up any secrets that may still stand in the way of intimacy (since intimacy is based on trust and honesty). For example, Ben's wife had an affair. Months after it was over, he asked her, "Did you really stop seeing Lennie when you said you did? I always had a sneaking suspicion that you saw him after that." She replied, "I was afraid to tell you then, but now I feel so safe with you. The truth is, I saw him several times more. I felt I couldn't end it except face to face, even though I promised you I'd do it by phone. And I did make love with him one last time—but it was so strange, it was like, all of the passion was gone. I think now I finally understand, the affair wasn't about him—it was about my disappointment in our marriage. And it was a stupid way to show my disappointment. I'm sorry for that, and I'm sorry that I lied."

Forgiveness is, to a large measure, a mutual act. When Ben heard Irene's admission and apology, something in him melted. Choking back tears, he asked her to accept his apology for having been so emotionally distant and preoccupied. "I guess we each played a role in this awful thing. I just pray we learned something from it, and we'll never have to go through this again."

There is still another aspect to forgiveness, a part that is not mutual, but private. Often, even years after an affair has ended, the involved partner still continues to feel profound guilt for the harm caused by the infidelity. It's as important to forgive yourself as it is to forgive your mate. Many of my patients find themselves focusing on the harm they caused. I ask them to also think of the good that came out of the pain. In almost every instance in which people get back together following an infidelity, the marriage is better than it ever had been. Going through the painful steps of recovery together develops a level of openness and communication that was unimaginable earlier in the marriage. I also remind guilt-ridden patients that they no longer need the guilt, since they have already used it to change themselves.

Similarly, the discovering partner also may harbor guilt. The most frequent thought is, "I got so tied up in everything but my relationship. I gave so much to the children, to my parents—there was nothing left for us. No wonder he went elsewhere." I point out the same thing to this patient—the learning has taken place—there is a new level of closeness. The guilt has served its purpose.

Forgiving for Divorcing Couples

Just as it is important for couples getting back together to reach a point of forgiveness, it is also a significant step for couples who must part. As I mentioned earlier, following an affair, many couples negotiate the three phases but still come to the conclusion that a divorce is inevitable. If they have gotten far enough to have explored what the problems in the marriage were, they too may be able to reach a point where they can have the closure that comes with forgiveness. Some divorcing couples, of course, are unable to reach a mutual closure, but many are able to within two to three years after the divorce.

Letting Go

Sometimes the discovery of infidelity is the prelude to a marriage ending badly, often with an all but complete breakdown in communication. Obviously, if this happens there can be no mutual forgiveness. If a partner leaves a relationship without ever having expressed admission or remorse, the other partner is left hanging. It is no easy task to gain closure when this happens. In such cases, it's important to find a way of letting go, lest the hurt and angry feeling that you are left with poison you emotionally.

Those who are familiar with twelve-step programs (such as AA) are aware of the concept of "Let go, let God." Before illustrating how the concept of letting go can be helpful, be aware that, to twelve-steppers, the term God doesn't necessarily mean the God of a particular religion. Rather, it refers to whatever a person thinks of as a higher power, or even the most noble part within the self. Letting go is not an angry act. Quite the opposite. It is an act undertaken in a serene fashion. It may take the form of a letter describing the impact of a person who has hurt you. Such a letter is written in "I" language, not the finger-pointing language of "you." Sometimes the letter is not sent at all. People have been known to bury letters or put them away in a special place. In my office there is a very special bowl, sculpted by a friend. Sometimes a patient, overcome by hurt that can never be corrected, writes down the pain on a piece of paper, crumples it up and places it in this very special bowl. This too is a form of letting go. People who can let go of profound hurts are able to move on to new and better parts of their lives. It is a skill worth cultivating.

Religious and Spiritual Values

If you are a religiously affiliated person, you may find great comfort in speaking with your clergyperson about how you are weathering this storm in your life. You may also find special comfort in attending religious services at this time in your life. Ironically, many people tend to avoid their religious institutions when they are in a marital crisis out of shame or out of a fear of somehow being judged. Most people report that if they do reach out, they find consolation and reassurance. In addition to the spiritual value of continued religious involvement, there is also a comfort that derives from fellowship and the familiar surroundings of your place of worship.

Networking

Peggy Vaughan is the author of *The Monogamy Myth* (1998). She describes the powerful effect of people joining together to share their experiences with infidelity. It is not only a source of information, but also a source of personal comfort. In her book she describes a network of groups (called BAN—Beyond Affairs Network) where people can gather to share thoughts and feelings about this topic. If you are computer-minded, you may find it very helpful to be in communication with others and to hear a variety of viewpoints. You will find a number of informational sites and many chat rooms. Many people especially like conversing on the Internet because it brings with it a welcome anonymity—most people don't use their real names, but instead go by a nickname, or by their e-mail address.

Healing

In this chapter we've examined many different paths to healing. Some relate to work that couples do together, whether they decide to work for a better marriage or to part. Some are of particular benefit to those who must face the end of their relationship alone. If there is a single principle that ties together almost every suggestion, it hinges on the increased ability to feel and to understand what you are experiencing. Another way of saying this is that you become more empathic with yourself. As this occurs, you also increase your ability to be empathic with your mate, if that person is willing to work through the pain and move toward a better marriage.

Remember

- You can survive infidelity either by achieving a more honest relationship or by leaving it wiser and better prepared for the next one

- Although affairs seem so intense and real, they are protected from most of the realities of your life, and so your thinking is distorted during an affair

- Accepting the possibility that there could be life after a divorce gives people the strength to honestly examine the marriage that they have and make good decisions about it

- Leaving a marriage because you believe your affair will become your next marriage is dangerous, because statistics say it probably won't be

- A healthy reason to end a marriage or a relationship is because, having given it your deepest thought, you know that it will never work

Children

What Children Require of Parents

Unfaithful behavior, like a powerful speedboat, leaves a wake behind it. Children, like small vessels, have been known to capsize in its churning waves. They crave the security that parents provide. They want to look up to their parents, seek their guidance, and see them as models of what is right. Seeing them as almost godlike, children need to believe in their parents' wisdom, even if they fight their authority. When parents fall short their children experience discomfort, disillusion, and confusion.

When adults are troubled, their children are often affected, no matter what their age. An affair that occurred even before a child's birth can later come to haunt him or her. Not only young children and adolescents, but also adult children and their marriages can be affected, although in different ways. The air of secrecy surrounding infidelity only serves to increase fear and suspicion. As children become aware that something is wrong (even though they may not know exactly what it is) they will have many questions. Among these are:

- I know something is going on—what's wrong?

- How bad is it?

- Are you trying to work it out?
- Will you divorce?
- What will happen to me?

These questions are not always directly communicated. They may instead find their expression in tantrums, anger, or depression that, on the surface, seem to have nothing to do with the infidelity. As a parent, you need to develop the skill of sensing what your child's behavior implies about what he or she is thinking and feeling. At times it's necessary for you to state clearly what you think your child is feeling. Questions, whether implied or stated, may require different answers, depending on the child's age and level of maturity.

While it is difficult for a couple going through a miserable time in their marriage to stop to consider how to help their children, it is profoundly important that they do. It has always impressed me that so many of the couples that I've treated for infidelity exhibit deep concern for their children and how they can best help them, even as they struggle to regain their own bearings.

Secrecy and Boundaries

A secret is information that is either kept from all others, or shared with some people and withheld from others. In order to talk about secrets as they relate to family life, you must begin by understanding another concept that is at the core of family therapy, namely, *boundaries*. Boundaries define the spaces between members of a family and between the family and the outside world. When things are going well in a family, certain boundaries are very clearly marked. For example, most families teach their children that some information is private, the exclusive property of the family, and not to be talked about with strangers. This constitutes a boundary, one side of which includes the family, the other, "outsiders." An example of a boundary inside the family is that oldest children are often given a certain degree of responsibility and power over their siblings when their parents are away from the house. However, when parents return, older children lose their power and are subject to their parents' authority, just as their younger siblings are. So we can see that boundaries define roles and rules in a family as well as levels of power. We would expect younger children to have less power and authority than their older siblings, and parents to have still more. But when boundaries are weakened, we may see reversals that undermine the family structure.

While children may feel uncomfortable and rebellious about parental authority, they nonetheless experience the emotional safety and security that is so much a part of healthy family life. Of course, the quality of their parents' relationship is very important to children. If their relationship is strong, parents function as a team and family relations are smoother; but if trouble (such as the discovery of infidelity) arises between parents, it reverberates throughout the family. One frequent result is the formation of new alliances amongst family members. An eldest child now may feel a duty to protect the parent whom they see as the injured party, and that parent may welcome and encourage the child's attention. Another child may feel hurt and excluded by this arrangement and become rebellious, or show discomfort in some other way.

Secrets have the power to disorganize family boundaries in a variety of ways. An involved parent may reveal information to a child, swearing the child to secrecy on the grounds that it would be too hurtful to the other parent to know. When this occurs, an appropriate boundary between parents and child is obliterated. With the new boundaries the child becomes allied through the secret with that parent and is put at a distance from the other. This can have profound effects on the child, who may feel very important (in fact, much too important) to the involved parent, but at the same time guilty about the disloyalty shown to the other parent.

Another form of boundary violation linked to secrets occurs when two or more children are told the secret separately, but each is pledged to secrecy. In this case, each of the children feels bound to the revealer of the secret, isolated from the opposite parent, and also isolated from one another.

How Secret Is a Secret?

The psychologist Mark Karpel (1980) has studied the impact of secrets on family life. Karpel points out that, "The confusion that surrounds secrets may make it difficult in some cases to make absolute distinctions between knowing and not knowing a secret." After a secret is revealed, people are likely to say that they suspected all along, or that they knew that there was some problem, but couldn't exactly identify it. It's probably realistic to assume that what you think of as a secret may be a partial secret, a secret to some but not to others, or no secret at all. Many children of families where an infidelity occurred tell me that the hardest part for them was maintaining the family secret. "It's like an elephant in the living room that no one felt they could mention," said one young man after his father had acknowledged his affair. "I knew it, my brother and sister knew it—I know that now, but I didn't know it then. At the time I thought I was the only one who knew. It wasn't even because I was told the secret—I just figured it out. Now, looking back, I think the only person who didn't know was Mom. It was so agonizing to hold this in all this time. I was afraid even to go to the guidance counselor to talk about how bad I felt. It was so strange. After all, I had already talked with the counselor about some real personal stuff, but I knew that you weren't supposed to talk about this, no matter what. And look how isolated it left my mother—we all knew, and she didn't."

Secrecy and Loyalty

If a child is the holder of the secret of a parent's infidelity, he or she feels sworn to silence. Karpel observes that "disclosing the secret would be experienced as an act of betrayal and would arouse guilt over the disloyalty." But just as children may feel guilt concerning the involved parent should they imagine revealing it, they may also feel that by *not* revealing it they are being disloyal to the parent who doesn't know. This guilt can go even deeper. Cal, a teenager, reported to me that his father took him out for lunch one day to introduce him to his girlfriend and told him that under no circumstances should he reveal this to his mother.

A few weeks later, his mother told him that she suspected that his father was having an affair and had hired a detective to follow him. She too swore him to secrecy. He felt that he had been carrying these two secrets reasonably well, until his older brother, a college student, returned home from school for winter break. Sensing the tension in the air, his older brother asked Cal if he thought there was anything wrong at home. Cal denied knowing anything, but feeling guilty, became very agitated, was unable to sleep, and lost about ten pounds in little more than a week.

His parents became concerned and spoke with the school counselor, who suggested that they and Cal see a family therapist.

At the very first session, it was only a matter of minutes before his father admitted the affair to his wife. As uncomfortable as it was to hear his father's admission, Cal felt greatly relieved. He no longer needed to carry this awful secret. It's not at all unusual for a child's symptoms to serve as a wake-up call to adults that it is time to bring an end to secrecy and to face the problems of the infidelity and the marriage head on.

Burdening Children with Adults' Issues

Discoverers often fear that their mate will abandon them for the third party. If the discovery doesn't lead to admission and remorse, this fear can become overwhelming. It can be followed by the suspicion that the children may also abandon them. In order to prevent this, the discoverer may then try to get the children to side with him or her. Reactions are varied. Some discoverers bad-mouth the involved partner, raising painful loyalty issues for the child. There may also be an excessive demand on children's time and attention, so that they come to feel that they have little life of their own. If a mother makes these demands on a teenage son, he may feel extremely threatened by what may seem to him a very uncomfortable degree of closeness. Many adolescent boys feel sexual overtones when there is any physical involvement, such as a demand for a hug or even too much "sweet talk." They may find it to be seductive and repulsive.

Adolescent girls may also feel an element of seduction in their fathers' attempts to gain favor with children whom they too fear losing. The fear of abandonment can lead a discovered male to actions that are equally upsetting to children. An adolescent girl in treatment with me received an enormous bouquet and a box of candy from her father on St. Valentine's day. She refused to accept them, and this led to a fierce argument between father and daughter. He insisted that his gift was just an expression of gratitude about how supportive she had been. At this point she threw the bouquet at him, screaming, "You idiot, can't you see that these shouldn't go to me—they should go to Mommy."

The children of philanderers are also locked in secrecy issues. Some philanderers make a particular point of bragging to their sons about their exploits. This can have two different consequences. Some boys identify with this part of their father and go on to become womanizers. Some sons discover their father's womanizing either by hearing about it from others or by directly observing it. A son who learns about his father's womanizing in this way is likely to be extremely repelled by it and feel very protective toward his mother. Most boys who are in this position keep this secret, confronting no one, because they find it so shameful. Nor is it only boys who suffer. Women who become Donna Juanas frequently had fathers who were Don Juans. It is also not at all unusual for the daughters of womanizers to marry womanizers.

Involving Children with the Third Party

Children are often unwittingly drawn into relationships with their parent's affair partners. For one thing, many affairs involve people who travel in the same social circle; for another, a good percentage of affairs are "office marriages." In either case, it's not unusual for the third party to be known to a child before the affair begins. When the involved parent finds ways to intensify the relationship between the child and the affair partner, the child generally has no idea that he or she is serving the parent's interest. It is only later that they become aware that they have been used.

One patient recalled his father's many affairs in the small town where they lived. "Where I grew up it was the custom to call most adults 'Uncle' or 'Aunt,' followed by their first name. This signified that they were, as my folks told me, 'like family.' This, of course, gave me a feeling of great trust and security—to know that there were all of these grown-ups around who cared for and about me. As I got older, I noticed that my father would seem to get particularly interested in one 'aunt' or another. As that happened, I would often find myself invited to join them for lunch at my father's office building, or to take a drive with them. One day, I observed my father kissing and hugging one of these women. I must have been about thirteen or fourteen. I thought I was going to die. Then I began to realize that each of these aunts was an affair partner. I felt paralyzed. I was unable to confront him, so throughout my adolescence, I bore witness to his affairs. I never was able to bring myself to talk to either him or my mother about it, but the thought was seldom far from my mind. I felt filled with anger and guilt. Worse still, I lost my faith in the decency of adults. I think the whole experience left me with two things: 1) I've never had an affair, and 2) I became a cynical and untrusting person. To this day, I find myself thinking, 'Who is?' and 'Who isn't?' I know it's also made me very overprotective of my daughters."

How Are Children Affected?

Parents often find that it is only an illusion to believe that they have kept an infidelity from the children. A former patient, four years beyond therapy, described this dilemma very well:

"As you know, the therapy went well, and we are happily back together. In fact, we're about to celebrate our twenty-fifth anniversary. One very important subject that we both had a great deal of difficulty handling was what would happen if the children found out what David had done. This didn't come up until six months after we stopped seeing you. David received a phone call from one of the women from his old job—where everything happened—to tell him that a relative of someone from work had died. I had picked it up, but Rachel, who was then ten years old, knew who this woman was. Rachel had occasionally gone to work with David, where she had met this woman, whom she had found to be pretty and charming. When she heard who was on the phone, she called out, 'Oh, Dad, your girlfriend is on the phone.' I was mortified, and we both said that Daddy didn't have a girlfriend. But Rachel answered that she knew he did. She told us that she could hear us talking about 'his girlfriend' (as I referred to her) when David and I would talk—usually very late at night. Obviously she somehow heard us and never said anything. Since she was young at the time I was able to make light of it (I told her that I was teasing Dad) but I have always worried that the truth would come out or that she didn't truly believe me. I didn't want my kids to know, since I felt that they would look at their father in a different, wrong light. During the bad times, I had a terrible relationship with our older daughter Leah, who was then sixteen, and I didn't want her using it as ammunition against him—at the time, I was the great protector. I'm still not sure that they didn't know, but since our marriage is good now and they can see it, I would never bring it up. Anyway, David and I both feel that protecting the children is something that should be dealt with from the beginning. Now we can see that we were so wrapped up in 'us' that we didn't realize that the kids were aware that something bad between Mommy and Daddy was going on. I thought we had kept things well hidden at the time, but now I know it shouldn't ever be talked about in the house (no matter what time it is) when the children are home. They're a lot smarter than we think."

Here is a young adult writing about her father's affair and her parents' subsequent divorce:

"I am a twenty-nine-year-old female who lived through my father's affair two years ago. It has changed my outlook on relationships, life, everything. I saw a side of my father that I never knew existed. I was my mother's confidant and therefore was told more than I would have liked to know. I felt caught in the middle, as if everyone needed me, but no one realized what I was going through. The experience has changed my relationship with my boyfriend. After eight years of dating, I still have no desire to be married and feel as if he will one day leave me as my father ended up leaving my mother. I have become very cynical. This experience has changed my outlook on life and relationships drastically. I suspect I'll never marry."

Having examined two cases in some depth, let's now look at some general guidelines about what to look for as children cope with this issue. You'll notice that in some instances two opposite behaviors are cited. This should come as no surprise. Stressful experiences often produce extremes of behavior.

Younger Children

Young children have not yet learned how to speak about complex and highly emotional issues. Because of this, they tend to show their emotional turmoil almost entirely through their behavior. Very young children will often show signs of insecurity and regression. For example, a toilet-trained four- or five-year-old may start having accidents. Children may suddenly become thumb suckers or nail biters. Clinging is not uncommon. Children who have always done well in school may show sudden declines in their school work or their school behavior. Some children develop frequent minor illnesses. Many have temper tantrums. Bad dreams and night terrors are often encountered. Some children set fires, others become the "perfect child."

Older Children

Older children may exhibit much of the same regressive quality seen in younger children. A major difference is that now they are capable of putting some of their feelings into words. Children of this age tend to be aware that tension between parents can be a sign that a divorce is coming. They know that their lives will be radically changed should that happen. While some will simply withdraw, others in this age group will say clearly how angry or frightened they are. Still others are not ready but show the same anxiety through talking in a fresh manner, acting extremely "hyper," and in every way they know how, attempting to make themselves seem so disturbed that their parents will realize that they must stay together. They may shoplift, vandalize, or begin getting into fights with other children. In some instances children in this age group threaten suicide.

Adolescents

Adolescents find it particularly hard to deal with infidelity. There are two reasons for this. First, they have just begun to develop the intellectual ability to see the larger picture. The great Swiss student of human development, Jean Piaget (for a good summary of his work, see Barry Wadsworth, 1971), described adolescence as the stage in a person's development during which reason and abstraction have developed to the point where intellectual maturity is achieved. Because they are equipped to look at the world in a critical manner, they can now examine the ideas and rules by which they are asked to live and test them against their own logic. For this reason, adolescents are exquisitely sensitive to "hypocrisy." Woe is the parent who asks an adolescent to do as he says, rather than as he acts—or even worse, the parent whose actions are opposed to his or her stated values.

Second, but equally important, adolescents are acutely aware of their budding sexuality. One moment they are irresistibly drawn to sex, and the next, repelled. In the orderly world that so many adolescents crave, they expect their parents to provide models of a secure relationship, one in which sexuality exists but within the family bounds.

Secrecy vs. Privacy

A secret is characterized by its "unspokenness." One way of distinguishing privacy from secrecy is that privacy can be declared. Asked about a certain incident or aspect of a person's life, the person might say directly, "I don't choose to talk about that. I consider it private." For example, if I'm treating a family, and parental issues like sexual dissatisfaction arise, I will ask the parents if they see this as a private matter, just between the two of them. If they agree that it is (and most people do), the children are asked to leave the room. This is not a secret. It is clear that they are having a problem. But they feel that it isn't information that is directly relevant to the children.

Dr. Karpel makes exactly this point as he distinguishes privacy from secrecy: "This distinction hinges on the *relevance* of the information for the unaware. A current secret extramarital affair by one spouse is, in most cases, highly relevant to the other spouse, because it involves major issues of trust and trustworthiness, deception, and a violation of reciprocity." Parents may need to think carefully about this distinction on the basis of relevance. For example, a parent may decide that a young child is not ready to know that one parent was unfaithful to the other but may be ready to know that, "as you can see, Mom and Dad have been fighting a lot—but we're trying to work it out." As the same child matures, the question may be of great importance as the adolescent struggles to understand relational issues. When this happens, parents may now decide to speak more openly with the child. Because they have reevaluated the information's relevance, they now feel ready to discuss this once private information.

You may now find yourself thinking, "Isn't this a boundary issue, too?" If you did, you'd be correct. When parents decide what is and isn't relevant to their children, they're showing them a boundary defined by adults' responsibility to protect children. It is within this protected space that children most easily grow and mature. For example, the parent described above who uses information about the other parent's affair to "win over" children is both violating a boundary and making something best kept *private* a *secret*. This may seem like simply playing with words, but it isn't. The parent must make an evaluation of the child's maturity and on that basis decide what will help the child to get through the crisis best. Telling the child that "Mommy and Daddy are having problems" is an honest report. It gives the child enough so that he or she doesn't feel excluded or "in the dark," but not so much that it is overwhelming. To say "there is no problem" would be a lie and would create an environment of secrecy. To say, "there is a problem" permits the parent to think, "Yes, but it's private—at least for now."

When to Speak to Your Children

Unless there is pressing need, it's not advisable to tell your children that an infidelity has occurred or is ongoing. If tension is evident between you and your spouse, children should be told that you are having a marital problem. If you feel that you're working hard to improve things, or if you are in therapy, they should be told that you're working hard so that things can get better. If they ask for more details, they should be told that the specifics are private. Sometimes the involved parent feels a need to tell children about the infidelity but has not yet admitted it to his or her partner. Under no circumstances should this be done. It puts the child in the unbearable position of holding an important secret.

There are certain circumstances, however, where it's impossible to offer children this degree of protection. One is if the two of you are openly fighting about the affair and the children hear accusations being hurled. Another is if there are rumors going around the community that the children are likely to hear. Certainly it would be better that they hear it from you before hearing it from outsiders. Another is if the affair has stopped, but the third party is engaged in stalking behavior. Finally, if the involved parent is contemplating moving out of the house and in with the third party, this too is best heard from the parents rather than strangers.

What to Expect When You Talk to Your Children

Because stability is so important for children, there is probably no way to start talking about an infidelity that will feel comfortable to them or you. After all, the thought that you are or were involved with another person, or that your partner is, represents the threat of great loss to the child. The best that can come of a first talk is that it will reduce the level of suspicion and plant the seeds for more successful conversation later on.

Younger children may appear uncomprehending when they hear that there is trouble in the family. Don't worry—they will take in as much as they are ready for, as long as you don't bombard them with gory details. Often, a younger child who at first seems unconcerned will later approach the parents with questions that show that the child indeed heard, but was not yet ready to talk.

Older children and adult children frequently respond angrily and are likely to be judgmental. They may have been suspicious for a while anyway, so admission gives them an opportunity to release pent-up hurt and anger. Everything that was said in earlier chapters about the response of the discoverer is applicable to older children. Thea, a fifteen-year-old, described her experience this way:

"My father took me aside one day to talk to me. I knew right away what he was going to say, because my Mom and Dad had been doing nothing but fighting for months, and you could hear right through the door that they were arguing about Millie. Millie is the lady who lives next door. She used to be Mom's best friend, and she was like an aunt to me and my little brother and sister. When my father told me, he was trying to be very nice and say all the right things. He spoke very quietly. He explained that he had already admitted it to Mom, and he wanted me to know that he was trying to end it, but he was still powerfully attracted to Millie. I couldn't believe it. The minute he said that, I started to scream at the top of my lungs. I'm a very polite person, but I called him the worst names I could think of. My throat hurt from screaming so loud. My face got so hot that it felt like my skin was going to burn off. He tried to get me to control myself, but I couldn't.

"I was relieved that I had a chance to let out some of what I had been holding in, and I guess it actually made me feel a little better that he had to humble himself by admitting it to me personally. I told him I thought he was a jerk and worse. I told him I couldn't believe he could do that to Mommy. And how dare he think so little of me and my little brother and sister?

"But that wasn't the whole story. As I fought with my father, it dawned on me that I was really very angry with my mother too. So I knew I had to sit down and talk to her too. How could she have taken all that crap and bullshit from my father? Did she really have any idea that it was going on, or for how long? As I listened to my Dad's story, it sounded to me like it had been at least two years. How stupid could my mother be that she didn't have any idea of what was going on. And if she did, what kind of a dishrag was she? How could she let herself be fooled that way—and by Millie? Her best friend?"

Thea then had a confrontation with her mother very similar to the one she'd had with her father. She really felt a little better after she had let out some of what she was feeling. She noticed that her parents began to treat her a little differently after her confrontation with them. They seemed to act as if she was a little more mature than they had thought.

Thea believed that one reason her parents stayed together might have been because she made such a point with her father about his irresponsibility. She says that she is relieved that they have stayed together. Too much in her life would have changed. Just fifteen years old, so many things were already changing for her—her school, her friends, even her appearance. A divorce, she said, would have been more than she could bear. Her father's affair didn't stop immediately after his admission. It was about two years before the affair was put to rest and her parents' relationship really showed improvement. Thea says that one of the best gifts she ever received was the day that her parents sat down with her and told her that they were really together for good.

Adult children often have particularly strong reactions. Keep in mind that parents are generally twenty-five or more years older than their children. Seeing the possibility of parents breaking up after perhaps forty years of marriage is very traumatic for many grown children. Many of them find that it stresses their own marriages as well. One man described his reaction when he heard that his seventy-year-old father had revealed a relationship with his secretary, a woman in her thirties. His first thought was, "She's younger than I am, younger than my wife!" Another was that this was probably not his father's first affair. He found himself reviewing years of his relationship with his father, his imagination running wild. Then he began to worry about what his responsibility would be toward his mother should their marriage end. Then he found himself feeling very shaky about marriage as an institution. The chain of thoughts was obsessive and endless.

Some adults have lived through a long history of parental infidelity, either in the form of affairs, serial affairs, or compulsive womanizing. Some authorities (Brown, 1991; Pittman, 1989) compare the effects of this sort of upbringing with that experienced by children who grow up in alcoholic or other addictive environments. Frank Pittman puts it this way: "The impact and the problems of people who grew up amid secrets and deceits and constant threats to the marital stability are not greatly different from those faced by children growing up with alcoholic parents." It is not unusual for people who have begun to piece together the impact of such a home on their lives (often through a combination of twelve-step work and therapy) to reach a point where they feel they must confront their parents. Even at this late date, parents who are ready to listen to and acknowledge their adult childrens' pain can begin the work of repair and healing.

Remember

- Children expect their parents to be models of honesty and consistency

- Parental problems cannot be easily hidden from children

- It is important for children that family boundaries be clearly set

- Children should not be burdened by secrets that are to be kept from siblings or the other parent

- Regardless of their age, it is usual for children to be deeply affected by a parent's infidelity

Family and
Friends

Seeking advice and comfort from family and friends is a chancy business. One may get more or less than one expected. When family and friends are supportive, they are a welcome source of solace and ideas. Often, however, the people to whom one turns are judgmental and opinionated. It is painful to seek help and feel turned away by criticism that seems unfair and unfeeling. In this chapter, we will examine the advantages and disadvantages of seeking this help.

Family

Jennifer was in the throes of coming to grips with her husband Ed's affair. She didn't know to whom she could turn to talk. She felt more alone and isolated than she had ever felt in her life. A rather private person, she at first resolved that, as lonely as she felt, it was still better to share this with no one. One day, visiting with her older sister Bernadette, she could no longer maintain silence. When Bernadette noticed how pale and quiet Jennifer seemed, she asked Jennifer if everything was all right. It was then that Jennifer began to sob and found herself describing her shock at Ed's behavior. As she dried her tears, she was amazed to hear her sister tell her that she couldn't help but notice that Jennifer had been yelling at Ed a lot recently. "Do you really think that's such a good idea?" she asked Jennifer. She went on to describe still other ways in which she felt Jennifer had been a deficient wife. Later Jennifer reported, "As close as I am to my sister, I regretted my poor judgment in talking with her and was bitterly disappointed in her for the way she responded to me. I went to her for a good ear and for some comfort, and I left feeling guilty and ashamed. I felt that she was really telling me that Ed's affair was my fault."

Long after Ed's affair was resolved and her marriage was going very well, Jennifer found herself thinking about her sister's response when she had tried to talk about the affair. Now, in a calmer state, she was able to see that Bernadette's response grew out of the way her sister and her sister's husband related to each other. Bernadette had always dealt with her husband's temperamental behavior by placating him. She always seemed to know when to back off. Jennifer could never remember even a single occasion when Bernadette had stood up to him. Perhaps that was the kind of marriage that Bernadette was comfortable in, but certainly it would not do for Jennifer. Because Bernadette had accepted her husband's moodiness without complaint, she expected no less of her sister and therefore could offer her no comfort.

Agendas

Jennifer's story is not atypical. When you approach family members, including parents and siblings, be aware that they may be speaking to you out of their own history, which may dictate how they will respond to you. Whether you come as the discoverer or as the involved person, you need to be aware of the agenda of the person with whom you are speaking. It is not easy for people to set aside their history, their values system, and sometimes, their fears.

Fantasies

When you share your situation with another person, it may trigger in that person's fantasies of what they wish they had done in a similar situation but never had the courage to carry out. Jill spoke with her mother about her passionate affair but also her confusion. She confessed that, while she felt madly in love with her affair partner, she realized that this was a temporary thing and believed that, given time, she would begin to feel once more the love that she felt she'd lost for her husband. She was shocked when her mother encouraged her strongly to continue the affair, even if it meant the end of her marriage. For nearly fifty years, Jill's mother had suffered through a difficult marriage. Jill knew that there had been occasions when her father had been verbally abusive with her mother. She had even seen him push and hit her a few times. As Jill talked more with her mother the story tumbled out. "So many times I prayed for the courage to get involved with someone else. I don't know why I've stayed all these years. Maybe I could have found love if I'd gone outside of the marriage." Jill felt that she had learned something new about her mother, but that her mother was so tied up in her own experience that she really couldn't be there for her.

Fears

Parents sometimes respond to the news of an affair with the fear that it will put greater responsibility on them if their child should divorce. Barry, whose wife was in an affair, turned to his parents to share his grief. To his shock, what he was told was to do everything in his power to keep the marriage together. "Don't count too much on us," he was told. His parents explained that they knew that a divorce would leave him pretty much broke, and dependent on them for help with his children and with finances. They made it clear that they didn't want that responsibility. Barry was deeply disappointed in his parents' response. He felt that he had come simply to share his concerns with them, not to request their help. Grandparents also worry that they will lose their connection to their grandchildren and even their son- or daughter-in-law if the marriage ends. Because of this, they may exert pressure on the child to stay in the marriage.

Parents Who See Children as Extensions of Themselves

Fearing that his wife was going to expose him to his parents, Gary decided that he should tell them before she got a chance.

Although he expected criticism, he was unprepared for his mother's reaction. "How could you do this to me?" For months following, she let him know how he was destroying her life. He felt that it was impossible for him to explain to her how frightened and confused he was. He was going to a therapist to try to work out his feelings, but so far, the more he talked to the therapist the more unsure he felt. Did he belong with this new woman, or was his place with his wife and children—or did he need more time alone for himself? There was no way to share this with his mother, who only saw her son's actions as an indictment of her as a mother. Gary felt that, in his mother's eyes, he had ceased to be a person in his own right. This served only to further confuse him.

Value Judgments

Parents' religious, cultural, or familial values may also make it difficult to turn to them for emotional support. You may hear: "This has never before happened in our family—we cannot tolerate it." Or, if you are the discoverer, you may be told, "You mustn't let this destroy your marriage—divorce is unthinkable, no matter what." Parents also may fear the shame that rumors about their children may bring to them. In extremely traditional religious groups, this fear may be all too real, bringing with it the threat of communal ostracism.

Side-taking

Consulting parents can have other unfortunate results as well. Frieda came to her parents, heartbroken, to tell them of her husband's recently discovered and still ongoing affair. Her parents, who had always been very fond of Harold, listened attentively. They appeared to be warm and supportive, calling almost every day to see how she was doing. Only gradually did she realize how angry and hurt they had been by Harold's actions. Frieda, however, had been advised by her therapist that this was probably a passing fancy for Harold, and her best bet was to keep off of the subject of the affair and focus on their own relationship. Since Harold seemed attentive when he was with her, and they continued a good love life, this seemed like a good strategy to her. But she discovered that her parents had become irrationally angry at Harold. Without ever openly alluding to his affair, they nonetheless did everything possible to indicate their disapproval. Even when things smoothed out between Harold and Frieda, her parents continued to treat Harold coldly. In the end, she wished she had never told them.

Supportive Families

There are, of course, many instances in which parents and siblings provide excellent support. Parents and siblings who wish to help will remember that there is a great likelihood that the marriage will survive the infidelity. For this reason, it is foolish to become judgmental, whether your loved one is the involved partner or the discoverer. They come to the family to be loved and to be heard. The best way to show this love is by doing a great deal more listening than talking. If you speak, it should be more to draw the person out, less to offer advice or opinions. Even if asked to make a judgment or give advice, the best course of action is to inquire more about how the person feels, or what the person thinks. Helping someone in distress to talk makes that person feel heard and feel better. The answers lie within the person, not within you. If you feel that you are in over your head, and that the person is terribly agitated or seems to be seriously depressed, it's worthwhile to suggest that perhaps speaking to a qualified therapist might be helpful. Chapter 11 has guidelines to assure finding a therapist who is competent with issues connected to infidelity.

Friends

All of the issues that have been discussed in terms of family relationships with infidelity-involved relatives also apply to their relationships with friends. These include fantasy, fears, value judgments, and side-taking. There are, however, some particular twists to these issues as they apply to friends, and some additional issues.

The Fear of Reaching Out

Both the discovering mate and the involved partner may feel extremely isolated as they face the problems that arise when infidelity comes to light. Because of the secrecy surrounding affairs and other types of infidelity, many people fear sharing their pain with any one and are likely to try to suffer it alone. This fear is not difficult to understand. First of all, what if one member of the couple or the other does reach out, and the person in whom they are confiding does not guard the secret? Second, what if the person who is taken on as a confidant is judgmental rather than accepting? Third, the discoverer may feel shamed and embarrassed at having been betrayed by a mate.

After years of secrecy, Alex finally admitted to his wife, Clara, that he had been sexually addicted for many years. He told her that he could no longer bear keeping this secret from her, and that the obsessional behavior that accompanied his addiction had brought him more and more down, until now he was contemplating suicide. Clara was disgusted by what Alex told her, and terrified of the possibility that she had contracted a sexually transmitted disease from him. Even more, she was enraged that for years he had dared to risk infecting her, even if he never had. How could he possibly love her and take such chances? He told her that he had already begun therapy, and that the first thing his therapist had told him was that he must join a Sexaholics Anonymous (SA) group. It seemed to him that none of this meant anything to her. She only asked that he get out of her sight. Desperate for a willing ear, he felt that he needed to talk with someone. As he went through his list of friends, he realized that there was absolutely no one he felt at all safe talking to. He called his therapist, who urged him to speak with no one but instead to attend an SA meeting and begin to find some fellowship there.

Clara refused to see Alex for over a month. When family and friends asked her what had happened, she simply told them that they'd had a falling out. She was feeling extremely alone—so ashamed and fearful of revealing this to anyone. There was one couple, Greg and Fran, to whom she and Alex had been particularly close. One day, unable to keep silent anymore, she revealed the truth to Fran. Fran was extremely supportive of Clara, who was enormously relieved. It felt so good to be able to talk to someone at last. Fran was as disgusted by what she heard about Alex as Clara had been. It was only later, when Alex and Clara reconciled, that Clara discovered that Greg and Fran would have nothing to do with them. When she confronted Fran, she was told that she had been a fool to go back to Alex—people like that never change, said Fran. Fran was angry with Clara, because she felt that she had made it amply clear to her how wrong she felt it would be for Clara ever to take him back. Why hadn't she taken her advice? Clara, in turn, felt betrayed by Fran. She believed that she had paid an unfair price for confiding in her.

Vicarious Interest

An affair often occurs when a person feels depleted and empty. The affair provides an excitement that fills the emptiness. Yet underneath the excitement and the infatuation lies profound ambivalence. As involved as the person is in the affair, there is often a part of the person that stands aside, as if it knew that the affair was not forever and that perhaps the marriage has an unrealized vitality. Because of this ambivalence, the affair-involved person is particularly vulnerable to the thoughts of valued others.

Peggy Vaughan, in her book *The Monogamy Myth* (1998), describes the impact that telling others often has on affair-involved women. "Most women only feel safe to tell their closest friends. But the reinforcement that comes from the excitement of telling others can increase the positive feelings about having an affair. And it sometimes carries the extra bonus of having her friends see her as a more interesting person because of this aspect of her life."

One reason that other women may respond by cheering on the affair is that they can vicariously experience the affair without the mess of having one themselves. One woman told me that, as she followed her friend's torrid affair, she felt as if her friend were the star of a movie, and that she was the costar. This reinforcement can have a powerful sustaining effect, maintaining the affair and blanking out the ambivalence, while never touching the underlying emptiness that the affair may be temporarily filling.

Friends in Whom You Can't Confide

On the other hand, friends may be extremely hesitant to even hear about an infidelity problem. This may be because they feel that their own marriage is in a brittle state, and they don't want their partner (or themselves) to think about doing anything that might make an already bad situation worse. Some people also fear that the discoverer has now become a threatening person, because he or she may be looking for a retaliatory affair.

Still other friends may have very strong feelings against either the involved partner or even the discoverer because of their own values about affairs. One patient of mine, a woman in her late twenties who thought that her marriage was excellent, was devastated when she discovered her husband's affair. She decided to turn to her best friend, just to talk about how she was feeling. Her friend told her, "Grow up and dry your tears. These things happen all the time." Later, my patient discovered that her friend was involved in an affair at the time. Sometimes the situation is even more painful. One woman called her best friend to say that she was having a marital problem. The friend replied, "I don't want to hear about it." Eventually it came out that this "best friend" was the one who was involved with the woman's husband.

The Effect of Social Isolation on the Involved Partner

While there are certainly good friends with whom one can talk, many involved partners are so absorbed in their affair and so afraid that someone might try to dissuade them from their infatuation, that they avoid talking with anyone in their circle of family or friends. They may then socialize exclusively with their affair-partner's friends. Earlier, I discussed the concept of the affair as a bubble, within which the affair couple floats, free of most adult responsibility. This new social circle may simply enlarge that bubble, yet at the same time intensify the involved partner's compartmentalization of the affair.

Marvin found himself in just this situation. After his affair with Zena began, he announced to Blossom, his wife of fifteen years, that he needed some time to himself. He denied that he was in an affair. He took an apartment. He came home frequently, remained a competent father to his two boys, and financially supported Blossom, just as he always had. But his emotional life was solely with Zena. The affair continued for close to five years. During that time Zena, who was single, had every reason to believe that Marvin would one day divorce Blossom and marry her. After all, didn't he attend her family affairs with her, and hadn't her circle of friends become his?

In Zena's circle, he was seen as a good guy. He liked the feeling so much. With Blossom and her family, he was seen as an abandoner, a person who could be most charming but was also capable of inflicting great hurt. In the extension of the affair bubble, Zena's family and friends reinforced the unreality of the affair and filled his emptiness nicely. It was only as his ambivalence resurfaced, and he decided to enter therapy with Blossom that Zena, her friends, and her family saw him in a new light—someone who, as they saw it, was cheating on Zena.

Marvin finally broke up with Zena. Looking back, he could see how the relationships that he had developed with Zena's circle maintained the illusion that he could successfully lead two lives. As he faced their disillusion and anger with him, he was finally forced to face himself and the emptiness that he had staved off for five long years.

Marvin and Blossom's therapist saw them not only as a couple, but also individually. In his individual sessions, Marvin came to understand the roots of his emptiness in the sad, distant home in which he had grown up. He had spent most of his life looking for easy ways to be liked by others. What he came to realize was that, as relationships became more complex (like his marriage) and he no longer felt always liked, he would immediately seek out the next place where he could feel absolutely accepted. He came to see how this made it impossible for him to ever reach a level of true intimacy, which sometimes involves accepting and responding to someone's real hurt.

Supportive Friends

Just as with family, supportive friends know how to be very good listeners. They work hard to help their troubled friend to hear him or herself better. They avoid making judgments about the other partner, because they know that there is a good chance that the couple will get back together, and their side-taking might only backfire. They are patient with their friend's indecision and ambivalence. They know that within a twenty-four hour period, a person who is frightened, angry, and confused may have changed his or her mind many times about whether to work through the problem or end the marriage. They also know when they are in over their heads, and their friend is bringing them problems that they feel unable to be helpful with. When this happens, they suggest that perhaps their friend might benefit from some professional counseling.

Finding the Right Person to Talk To

It is, of course, important to find somebody trustworthy with whom you can talk about this painful situation. A supportive person will do much more listening than talking—drawing you out so that you begin to hear your own feelings, and especially your ambivalance, more clearly. A good listener is attentive and empathic. Whether friend or parent, a good listener is supportive but is careful not to badmouth your partner. They instinctively sense that, if you get back together, their side-taking will become a source of problems later on. A supportive person is extremely trustworthy. You feel absolutely sure that such a person will not gossip to others about your situation. If you think that you've found the right person to talk to, perhaps you might want to describe what you've learned in this chapter about supportive families and supportive friends. You can explain that there is something very sensitive you'd like to talk about, but that you want to be as sure as possible that this is a responsibility the person can (and is willing to) take on.

If there is no one in your circle who truly fills that bill, it is still important to find someone with whom you can talk safely. One possibility is through a support group. This may be done through a community center, a "Y" group, or by contacting your local Mental Health Association. Of course, it may be extremely valuable for you to contact a therapist who is qualified to help you with this problem. Chapter 11 deals with how to find the right therapist.

Remember

- The advice of friends and family may be colored by their own situations or history

- A friend or family member can help most by being a good listener

- Talking to those who hear you without judging or offering unsolicited advice can help you to clarify your thinking

- Sometimes seeking professional help is the best way to go

Is It Always
Best to Tell?

Given the fact that so much of this book has dealt with the trauma of discovered infidelity and the problems inherent in maintaining secrets, it may seem strange that the question, "Is it always best to tell?" should even be raised. From a theoretical position, the answer seems clear enough. If you want a relationship that is truly close and intimate, honesty and openness are necessary ingredients.

The trouble is that people are not theories. As I have watched clients struggle with the issue of if and what to tell, I have come away with a deepened respect for the complexity of the issue. Let me begin with a story. John and Arlette had seen me many years ago. At the time he had been involved in an intense affair which he absolutely denied when Arlette challenged him. After a few weeks of denial, John admitted to and then ended the affair. It had not been his first, and he admitted this too. They spent some time in therapy talking deeply about their marriage, and each took some mature responsibility for how distant they had grown from one another by the time the affair had begun. When they completed therapy, both agreed that their marriage was the best and most intimate that it had ever been. Arlette made it absolutely clear to John, however, that if it ever happened again, the marriage was over. A number of years later, John called to ask if he could see me alone. He came to tell me that he felt, as he said, "As if I'd come as close to the edge of the cliff as you can go without falling off." He had found himself drawn increasingly to a young colleague at work, and after a few weeks, he took her out for lunch and then to a nearby hotel, where they had sex. While in the past, he said, he would have considered this simply an exciting dalliance, this time he was overcome with guilt about what he had done. The second it was over, he said, all that he wished was that it had never happened. "What a fool I feel like," he said. "After everything I learned in therapy, how could I have thought that the second's pleasure that I might get from this was worth endangering my marriage?"

The more I listened to John, the more convinced I became that this had been a turning point for him. The psychological study of how we learn teaches us that there is a special type of learning that comes from fearsome experiences. The way children learn to avoid hot stoves, unfortunately, is often by touching one. Once they have, they have also learned not to do it again. My sense was that John had touched the hot stove, and had learned.

John's question was this: "I know that I've changed. I know in my heart that it will never happen again. I believed Arlette when she told me that if it happened again it was over, and I still do. I'm afraid that if I tell her, I will have destroyed the thing that means the most to me."

I asked John if he felt that he had learned anything from this experience other than not to do it again. "Yes," he replied. "I think that I get tempted when I am going though a very stressful period at work. I've noticed myself being tempted at other times since we ended therapy, and always for this reason. I also know that, macho man that I still am, it has been my tendency not to talk to Arlette about my stresses. So, I think what I've learned is that if I'm getting stressed out, I have to share it with her and not try to shield her from it. Then the erotic charge I got from the flings would get put back where it belongs, between me and Arlette."

John decided in this instance not to tell, but to take personal responsibility for continuing to grow in his marriage. Of course there were dangers in his decision, and they were not far from John's mind. The young woman with whom he got involved was an assistant to him. What if she got it into her head some day to bring him up on charges of sexual misconduct? What if he had contracted a disease and passed it on to Arlette? The second was easy enough to check. He consulted with his physician and received a clean bill of health. As to the first, he said, "I think it's a risk I'll have to take. If I told Arlette, I think it would guarantee that the marriage would be over. The likelihood that I'll get sued by this woman is tiny. I'm trained in business. My business sense says it's a risk worth taking." Clearly this was not a decision taken lightly. As John said, "Last time, my affair was a secret against Arlette and against the marriage. This time, I feel I must hold this secret *for* the marriage."

Telling When Asked

What if the situation had been somewhat different? Let us assume that Arlette had once again become suspicious and directly asked John if he was playing around again? I asked John what he would do in that case. "Now, or much later, way after the fact?" he asked. "Let's think about each case," I replied. "Well," he said, "if it was as it was happening, I would have to admit it. I know that my lying about it, in the face of her fears, was what drove her into near insanity last time. I just couldn't ever do that to her again. I would try to explain to her what I've explained to you, and just pray that it would help her to begin to trust me again. But it could blow up and that might be the end. I hate to even think of it. And later—that might be a little safer. I think if it was years later and somehow it came up, we'd have all those good years built up. I guess she'd see by all my actions in the ensuing years that I really had changed. Then maybe the slate would be clean, and she could forgive me. But as things stand, I think I have to go to my grave with this."

Telling When Not Asked

There are a variety of opinions concerning whether to tell if you are not asked. Frank Pittman contends that, whether the infidelity is in the present or the past, it is wisest to reveal it, because he feels that marriages that avoid issues are weakened by the dishonesty. Secrets, he remind us, keep people at a distance from one another. Fred Humphrey (quoted in Dalma Heyn's *The Erotic*

Silence of the American Wife, 1997) says: "I've worked with lots of couples where the affair was kept secret, who decided to end the affair and then put all their energies in the marriage." Humphrey believes that, in some cases, honesty backfires, and the memory of the affair never goes away for the discoverer, who may also then use it as a way of retaliating later in the marriage.

It is helpful, if you are thinking about revealing a long-held secret, to consider the following questions in order to be clear about what you hope to accomplish by your admission.

- To get it off my chest
- To improve communication
- To hurt the other person
- As a way of forcing the other to ask for a divorce

If you are considering sharing an old secret, use your journal to analyze why it interests you to do it at this particular time. You may have other reasons as well, and they too should be written down and explored. If you are feeling conflicted about whether to tell or not, use the "best–worst" format described in chapter 4. This same exercise will be helpful at other points in this chapter as well.

A man in his seventies found himself thinking more and more about an affair he had when he was in his midthirties. It was around the time of the Jewish High Holy Days, a time when people are asked to look into themselves, and seek forgiveness for wrongs that they have done. He was feeling a strong desire to reveal this secret that he had carried for so long to his wife of fifty years. He decided to speak with his rabbi, who had known them for many years, before taking any action. The rabbi asked him what he hoped to accomplish by telling her. He replied, "It would make me feel better." The rabbi asked that he carefully consider how it would make his wife feel. The man decided that it would make her feel terrible and accomplish nothing. It certainly wouldn't make him feel better if it made her feel worse. His decision was made.

The Dangers of "One Size Fits All"

Most of us have had the experience of buying some article of clothing labeled "one size fits all." Often, we find that it really doesn't. Much of the advice that we read about whether or not to admit to an infidelity is of the "one-size-fits-all" variety. For example, in his book *Marital Myths* (1985) the psychologist Arnold Lazarus argues that one of the false beliefs that people accept about marriage is: "If you feel guilty, confess." By referring to this belief as "false," he implies that, if possible, infidelity should never be revealed to a spouse. He holds that while, in a really deep friendship, you can talk about anything, that this is not the case for marriage. Certain information, he states, can "overload" a marriage. Revelations about extramarital involvements—be they one-night stands or enduring passionate affairs—fall into this overload category. He then proceeds to tell three stories about men (no women are included) who do tell and then suffer great consequences, in some cases unwanted divorces.

The writer Dalma Heyn, mentioned earlier, writes specifically about women and their affairs. She cites a number of authorities who support the statement that "for women who confess, divorce rather than reconciliation is the more likely outcome." She holds that this is an important reason for the reluctance of many women to admit to infidelity.

The problem with these blanket statements is that they ignore important distinctions. There is a big difference between offering up an unrequested confession and admitting the truth when you are directly asked. Lazarus's "myth" and the observations quoted by Heyn do not tell us what type of admission is being talked about. A general rule such as, "under no condition admit guilt," simply doesn't cover both. I have seen marriages considerably worsened because a partner felt the necessity to unburden her- or himself about an old and unsuspected transgression. On the other hand, there is no situation that I know of that is *improved* by continuing to lie once a direct question is asked. Going back to Arnold Lazarus's advice never to tell: he lumps together one-night stands and lengthy affairs. These are in fact two radically different types of infidelity, since one involves an emotional attachment, and the other doesn't. He also doesn't specify whether what is not to be admitted to is in the present, the immediate past, or the distant past. He also tells us nothing about whether the partner suspects or not. In order to make a reasoned decision about such an important action, all of these questions require consideration.

Dangerous Mates— a Special Case

In one very special case there are compelling reasons to lie for the sake of self-preservation, even if you are barraged with questions. Notice: this will not improve your marriage, but it might save your life. In order to determine whether you are in this special situation, key questions must be answered: "Is my mate a dangerous person? Is he (or she) likely to inflict serious physical harm on me or even possibly murder me? Is my mate likely to attempt to destroy me financially if I should admit it?" It is important to distinguish these security- or life-threatening fears from what we know will probably happen in any relationship when an ongoing infidelity is admitted. We expect a strong emotional reaction whenever a person feels betrayed, as described in earlier chapters. But the kind of violence we're talking about here has a very different quality than the usual reaction following an emotional trauma. If patients tell me that should they answer a question about infidelity their life would be in danger, I ask them how rapidly they can find shelter elsewhere, how quickly they can get legal advice, and whom they can count on as a support network. Why would anyone willingly remain in such a dangerous environment? (Of course there are answers to that question, but they will be found in books about battered women—they are beyond the scope of this book.)

Another Special Case

It is my own strong belief that, in most cases, if people are asked, they should answer honestly. The exceptional cases include the possibility of violence, and the unusual set of circumstances detailed below.

Jed was a highly successful divorce attorney. When I treated him and Ruth for marital problems, I began to suspect that he was involved in an affair. It's my practice to meet with each member of the couple alone early in the marital therapy, and before I do so, I explain that there will be absolute confidentiality in any meeting with only one person. That means that the person is free to talk with the partner about the session, but I will not. Because of this guarantee, people are remarkably honest in these meetings. Jed admitted that he had been involved in a lengthy affair and was still confused about whether he wanted to end the marriage or not. Based on that meeting, I continued to see him alone, because he couldn't devote sincere energy to the marriage. He agreed, and I continued to see Ruth alone as well. Eventually Jed came to the conclusion that he was finished with the affair and asked to return to marital therapy with Ruth. I asked him whether he felt ready to explain to Ruth what had happened, and he refused. "I know on some theoretical level your reasons are very compelling," he told me. "But you've got to remember that I'm a lawyer, and a divorce lawyer at that. If a client told me she or he was going to admit to something, I would tell them—don't. And I won't."

In her individual meetings, Ruth had never mentioned even the slightest suspicion that Jed had been having an affair. Nor did she when they returned to sessions together. I kept waiting for her to ask him, but it never happened. Meanwhile, they worked very spiritedly and creatively on their marriage and were doing better every week. Until one week, when she requested an individual session. "I'm not a fool, you know," she told me. "I know that he's been playing around. I also know that he'll never tell me—he's a lawyer, you know. But I believe he realizes that all those sessions you two guys had alone tipped me off to what was going on. I've decided that we have a good thing going in our marriage, so I'm going to focus on that and let go of his affair. The funny thing is—I'd swear he knows that I know."

In chapter 1 I mentioned the concept of arrangements—situations in which two people agree openly that an affair is within their rules for the marriage, so that it is not a potentially toxic secret. I also mentioned that some people never openly discuss this, but it is a covert agreement about their relationship. I believe that Jed and Ruth came to a covert agreement to put aside the affair and concentrate on improving their marriage. It certainly worked for them.

Recent Infidelities

There are a number of cases other than long-term infidelity where the issue of whether or not to tell requires attention. Let's focus now on recent incidents, including brief affairs, one-night stands, or experimentation with prostitutes.

One important question to ask yourself is: "Even if I have stopped this practice, how much risk have I put my mate at?" If you had your choice, would you prefer that your mate learned what you had done because you told him or her, or because they discovered that they had an unexplainable case of some sexually transmitted disease? Another question you might ask yourself is, "Even if my brief affair is over, would it be better for my mate to hear it from me, or through hearsay?" Remember, once you are confronted, the probability that you will successfully lie your way out of it is very small.

Sexual Addictions

If you have admitted to yourself that you have a sexual addiction, then you have also come to realize how it is disrupting not only your life, but your partner's life as well. It's going to be a long road back, and you will probably require both individual therapy and group work. If you don't tell your spouse about the addiction, how will you cover up such a commitment of time? Do you see some advantage in sharing your new understanding with your mate? Do you believe that, following the inevitable emotional reaction to this news, you will feel more or less close to your spouse than you do now?

From Painful to Positive

The decision about whether or not to tell and how to tell if you decide to, is not an easy one. In this chapter, you've seen that various authorities have remarkably different ideas about what works and what doesn't, what might improve your relationship and what might cause an unwanted breakup. This places a remarkable degree of responsibility on the involved partner. Perhaps the most important guideline to remember as you make your decision is: How can this painful situation serve a useful purpose in your relationship? Sometimes this is best accomplished by owning up to your actions. Sometimes it involves keeping something private but experiencing a deep internal change that brings you back to the relationship as a better partner. Sometimes honest admission paves the way for a decent parting.

Remember

- If you are directly asked, whether about a present or a past infidelity, it is best to answer honestly—unless you fear bodily harm

- If you're thinking about revealing "ancient history" when you've not been asked, examine your motives carefully before doing so

- If you are engaged in risky behavior, you are endangering your mate's health by not revealing it

- If you do reveal something, try hard to keep the focus on how and when you lied, not on the gory details

- Whether or not you decide to reveal or to live with a secret, use the experience to help you to change you relationship

Choosing a
Competent Therapist

What Is a Therapist?

Working your way through infidelity often requires the help of a qualified therapist. A therapist is a person who is trained to help people deal with emotional problems. Unfortunately, in most states anyone can put up a sign saying that that he or she is a therapist, counselor, or psychotherapist. People who do this are not covered by any state board or any national association's ethics rules. For that reason, it's important to understand what a *qualified* therapist is: a person who is trained and licensed to help people deal with emotional problems.

There are a variety of people who are trained and licensed as health providers whose specialty is mental health. In most states these include psychologists, psychiatrists, and social workers. In some states there is a separate license for family counselors. If you choose to seek guidance through a religious institution, you should know that pastoral counselors are generally not licensed, but may have received good training at their seminary or at some other institution and have a certificate showing this. But remember, beware of unlicensed therapists or counselors. In this chapter, the term therapist should always be taken to mean a licensed person who practices psychotherapy.

What Is Family Therapy?

All therapists receive training in individual therapy. Unfortunately, many therapists have little if any training in family and couples therapy, which is a very specialized form of therapy. So one of the things that you need to know about a potential therapist is whether she or he has postgraduate training in family therapy. Family therapists are trained to see two or more members of the family at the same time. The theory and the skills that help therapists do this kind of work differ somewhat from those that guide people who do only individual therapy. This means that when you are checking on a particular therapist, you will want to ask what additional training the person obtained in family therapy.

Even if you feel that you need to see a therapist about some aspect of infidelity alone, without your partner, it is still best to choose a family therapist for two reasons. First, a family therapist is more likely to be knowledgeable about family life and infidelity than a therapist with only general training. Second, should you wish to include your partner later on, the family-trained person will know how to make this switch from seeing you as an individual patient to treating you as a member of a couple.

Finding a Therapist

One good way to find a therapist is to talk to friends and neighbors. If someone has used a particular therapist and found him or her to be helpful, you may feel encouraged to try that person yourself. If your contact is willing to speak openly with you, you should ask whether the person was seen alone or for couples therapy. If your contact knows the qualifications of the therapist, that may tell you whether it's worth having a meeting with the therapist.

The telephone is always a good instrument for quickly gathering information. If you call the national offices of the American Psychological Association, for example, they will give you the number of the local county psychological association, who can give you a list of therapists in your geographic area who are specialized in marriage and family work. The American Association for Marriage and Family Therapy will provide you with a similar service. Both organizations are located in Washington, D.C. Your local Mental Health Association is also a good source of information. There are also counseling centers and hospital outpatient mental health centers in most communities. These services are often offered on a sliding fee scale. Many of these centers will say that they offer family therapy (couples counseling is considered to be a type of family therapy). Be sure to raise the same questions if you are contacting a clinic that you would ask of a therapist in private practice.

Seeing Two Different Therapists

I am often asked about the advisability of each member of the couple seeing his or her own therapist when the marriage is in crisis. There is some evidence that it's wiser to find one therapist to treat the couple. If you see your own therapist, that person will struggle hard to enter into your world, to see things through your eyes, and to empathize with your position. If each of you is seeing a therapist who works this way, you may find yourselves being drawn still further apart. This may entrench each of you in your own position and make dialogue between you even harder.

A Phone Meeting

If you are able to reach the person you're considering seeing by telephone, this gives you an opportunity to speak about why you're coming and to inquire about the therapist's training in general, particularly about his or her experience in dealing with marital infidelity. You will probably finish that conversation with an intuitive feeling about whether or not you would be comfortable working with this person. Seemingly silly things can be really important to you. A friend of mine told me that she had contacted a therapist whom I had suggested to her. When she spoke with him on the phone, she said that he spoke so quickly that it took her breath away. When she recounted this to me, I told her he might talk fast, but he often had very good things to say. Taking my suggestion, she and her husband went for a first meeting with him. On the way home both agreed that he spoke so quickly that it made them nervous, and they also found it hard to follow what he was saying. It was probably the first thing they had agreed on since the infidelity had come to light. They had to find a different therapist.

Interviewing the Therapist

The first meeting with a therapist following the discovery of infidelity is a very difficult one for both of you and for the therapist as well. About ten or fifteen minutes before the session's end, many therapists will ask you something like this: "You know, I've had to ask you two lots of questions today, and I believe this has been a tough session for both of you. I've left a few minutes now for you to ask questions that you have about me, about my training, and about how I'm working with you." It's a good idea to agree before the first meeting that if the therapist doesn't suggest some time to talk about these things, that one of you will raise the question. This is your opportunity to ask questions like: "How would you describe the kind of therapy you do? Have you worked with many cases that involve infidelity? Have you had special training in infidelity?"

Don't be inhibited about your questions. Ask what you feel you need to know about. Some people ask me, for example, how old I am, if I'm married and for how long, if I have children and grandchildren, and sometimes even if this is my only marriage. These questions might seem a bit nosy to some, but to me they indicate that the couple wants to know if I can be trusted with their marriage. I've often wondered what the reaction would be if I were to say one day, "Well, I'm on my fifth marriage and still in there trying."

How Do Couples Therapists Work?

If there is one thing about which all schools of couples therapy agree, it's that the therapist must begin by making a series of alliances early in the therapy. The work of Alan Gurman (1982) details three such alliances. The first is with each member of the couple as a unique human being. An alliance must also be made with these two people as a couple. Finally, the therapist needs to create an alliance with the couple in their roles as husband and wife. Let's take a look at how each of these alliances work.

The alliance with each marital partner as a unique human being. By the end of the first meeting with the therapist, each of you should feel that you've gained something of personal value to you from the therapist. This might be as simple as empathy. The way the therapist responded to a particular feeling you expressed lets you know that you were being heard. You might notice that, as you talked over your feelings about the therapy afterward, you both agreed that neither of you was favored over the other.

The alliance with the couple. Just as you each should have the feeling that, both literally and figuratively, the therapist can look at you as two unique people, you also should have the sense that she or he can look at you as a couple. When the therapist is doing this, the focus is not on each of you as individuals, but what is happening between you. For example, the therapist might mention that, as angry as you are with each other at the moment, still you're looking very attentively at each other and listening with every fiber of your beings. This is a remark directed not alone at either one of you, but to an aspect of your relationship. As Dr. Gurman says, "The therapist must learn to speak to both spouses at the same time."

The alliance with the couple as husband and wife. The therapist also must focus on the particular roles that you take as husband and wife. It is very common for a couple who come to therapy in a crisis to be very aware of how different they are from each other and how much conflict they are experiencing. The therapist works to help the couple understand that at the moment, their conflicts are the best way they know to try to achieve what most couples want—emotional companionship. A couple who have not yet come to peace with issues related to the homes in which they grew up often come to therapy able to connect more through conflict than through healthier forms of emotional sharing. If the therapist is successful in helping you understand this dynamic, you will feel that you are learning something important about how your roles have meshed to create what you are now as a couple. You will also sense that, with work, there is hope for genuine change.

Clear Procedures

Your therapist should make clear to you his or her procedures for conducting therapy. For example, what the fee will be, if the therapist can accept your insurance assignment and if there's a co-payment. What will happen if you have to cancel a meeting; what happens if only one of you is available at the scheduled time—if that person should come alone; what the rules of confidentiality are if one of you comes alone; if the therapist will feel free to tell your partner what you talked about when you came alone; if it's your therapist's goal to keep your marriage together, or if he or she will help the two of you to reach your own conclusion and help you to carry it out; what the therapist would consider to be a good outcome of the therapy if you separated; if there's any point at which the children might be included in the therapy. You may think of other important questions either before you come to a session or after you've left. It's important to jot them down so you can ask your therapist. A competent therapist welcomes your questions.

Continuity in Treatment

After a few sessions, you should notice that you have a sense of continuity about your work from one session to the next. For example, if you ended a session in which one of you was just beginning to talk about some very important aspect of your life growing up (for example, an alcoholic parent, the death of a sibling, frequent moves) you would have reason to expect that the therapist would pick up on this at the beginning of the next session. If the therapist has given homework (for example, the journal writing in this book), is it followed up on at the next meeting? Of course, if you come in with a crisis, sometimes this continuity is better postponed, but a competent therapist will try to come back to the assignment as soon as possible.

You Are a Partner with
Your Therapist

You're coming to therapy to consult about a particular problem. If one or both of you are beginning to feel uncomfortable with how the therapy is progressing or are upset with or do not understand something that the therapist did or said, it's most important that you voice that concern. For example, you may be upset about your therapist's accepting a phone call during your session. You need to discuss his or her policy about this openly, and then decide whether you can live with it. You may feel that the therapist is siding too much with one of you. The therapist needs very much to know if you're seeing this. In short, any discomfort either of you have should be shared. If one of you says to the other, "I'm not going to come back after this session," you should urge him or her to return for at least one more time and talk about it at the beginning of the session. You may even wish to bring it up yourself if your partner refuses to. After all, if your therapist wants you to become better communicators with each other, certainly the therapy needs to be conducted by the same rules. If your therapist becomes defensive and annoyed if you raise questions, you may need to consider whether you have the right therapist for yourselves.

If Therapy Is Not Going Well

You always have the right to end therapy with that particular person and find someone else. Sometimes a bad experience with a first therapist will help you develop a clearer idea of what you're looking for and help you make a better decision on the next try. But before you decide to end therapy, it's wise to speak with the therapist about your concerns. After all, you've already invested time and energy, and it's sometimes a bit discouraging to contemplate starting over with someone new. One thing you might do is ask the therapist to review the case with you, so you can discuss what seems to be going wrong. Many therapists welcome a consultation with a respected colleague about a complex case. Some therapists will consult with this person and then bring back that person's observations to you. Some will suggest that you meet with another expert for a consultation about the course of therapy. In some instances, a therapist will, with your permission, invite a colleague to observe a session and make some suggestions about how to improve the situation. Most competent therapists want very much to know how you feel the collaboration with them is going and will welcome one of these suggestions as a good way to break the impasse.

If all avenues have been tried and one or both of you continue to feel the therapy is not helping, it is urgent to make a change. Doing this is no reflection on you, and perhaps not on the therapist either. Sometimes there is simply a poor match.

Remember

- You have entered therapy for help based on experience, training, and caring—if any of these are missing, find another therapist

- Your therapist's procedures should be explained to you clearly

- You are in a collaboration with your therapist—the therapist is not your boss

- If you attend therapy together, you should each feel fairly heard and fairly treated

Some Final Words

In the introduction to this book, I described a sign in my waiting room with the Chinese symbol for the word "crisis." Beneath the symbol is the explanation that the symbol consists of two words, one signifying "danger," and the other, "opportunity." It is my hope that as you read this book you found an opportunity for growth in this stressful time. As you read these final words, you are most likely already on the way to a better relationship than the one that preceded the discovery of the infidelity. You may have discovered new resources in yourself and your loved ones beyond what you might have ever imagined.

For some, a break up appears inevitable. It's my hope that those of you who face divorce can end your marriage in a way that's fair to each partner, and, for those of your with children, in a way that especially respects them. Most important, I hope that you have developed a better understanding of what went wrong in your relationship, and that you have developed new insights that will help you move to a new one that benefits from what you've learned.

For some of you there may still be no resolution. I urge you to get the help you need, both as individuals and as a couple, so that you can bring the situation to an end that benefits both yourselves and your children.

References

Ahrons, Constance R. 1994. *The Good Divorce*. New York: Harper-Collins.

Beck, Aaron. 1988. *Love Is Never Enough*. New York: Harper & Row Publishers.

Brown, Emily. 1991. *Patterns of Infidelity and Their Treatment*. New York: Brunner/Mazel, Inc.

Carnes, Patrick. 1983. *Out of the Shadows: Understanding Sexual Addiction*. Minneapolis, Minn: Compcare Publications.

Earle, Ralph, and Gerald Crowe. 1989. *Lonely All the Time: Recognizing, Understanding and Overcoming Sex Addiction, for Addicts and Codependents*. New York: Pocketbooks.

Ellis, Albert. 1975. *New Guide to Rational Living*. California: Wilshire Book Co.

Flach, Frederic. 1988. *Resilience*. New York: Ballantine Books.

Frankl, Victor. 1976. *Man's Serach for Meaning*. New York: Pocket Books.

Glass, Shirley, and Thomas Wright. 1992. "Justifications for Extramarital Relationships: The Association between Attitudes, Behaviors, and Gender." *The Journal of Sex Research* 29: 361–387.

Gurman, Alan S. 1982. "Creating a Therapeutic Alliance in Marital Therapy." In *Questions and Answers in the Practice of Family Therapy, Volume 2,* edited by A. S. Gurman. New York: Brunner/Mazel.

Heyn, Dalma. 1997. *The Erotic Silence of the American Wife.* New York: Plume, a Division of Penguin Books, USA, Inc.

Humphrey, Fred. 1987. "Treating Extramarital Sexual Relationships in Sex and Couples Therapy." In *Integrating Sex and Marital Therapy: A Clinical Guide,* edited by G. Weeks and L. Hof. New York: Brunner/Mazel.

Janoff-Bulman, Ronnie. 1992. *Shattered Assumptions: Towards a New Psychology of Trauma.* New York: The Free Press.

Karpel, Mark. 1980. "Family Secrets: I. Conceptual and Ethical Issues in the Relational Context." *Family Process* 19:295–301.

Kaslow, F., and H. Hammerschmidt. 1992. "Long Term 'Good Marriages': The Seemingly Essential Ingredients." *Journal of Couples Therapy* 3:15–38.

Lawson, Anette. 1988. *Adultery: An Analysis of Love and Betrayal.* New York: Basic Books.

Lazarus, Arnold. 1985. *Marital Myths.* San Luis Obispo, Calif.: Impact Publishers.

Lerner, Harriet Goldhor. 1985. *The Dance of Anger.* New York: Harper & Row, Publishers.

Levant, Ronald, and Gary Brooks. 1997. *Men and Sex: New Psychological Perspectives.* New York: John Wiley and Sons, Inc.

Levinson, Daniel. 1978. *The Seasons of a Man's Life.* New York: Alfred A. Knopf.

Lusterman, Don-David. 1997. "Repetitive Infidelity, Womanizing, and Don Juanism." In *Men and Sex: New Psychological Perspectives,* edited by R. F. Levant and G. R. Brooks. New York: John Wiley and Sons, Inc.

———. 1989. "Marriage at the Turning Point." *Family Therapy Networker* 13:44–51.

———. 1995. "Treating Marital Infidelity." In *Integrating Family Therapy: Handbook of Family Psychology and Systems Theory,* edited by R. Mikesell, D-D. Lusterman, and S. McDaniel. Washington, D.C.: American Psychological Association.

Masterson, James. 1988. *The Search for the Real Self.* New York: The Free Press.

Philpot, Carol, Gary Brooks, Don-David Lusterman, and Roberta Nutt. 1997. *Bridging Separate Gender Worlds: Why Men and Women Clash and How Therapists Can Bring Them Together.* Washington, D. C.: American Psychological Association.

Pittman, Frank. 1987. *Turning Points.* New York: W. W. Norton & Co., Inc.

———. 1989. *Private Lies.* New York: W. W. Norton & Co., Inc.

———. 1993. *Man Enough.* New York: G. P. Putnam's Sons.

Sartre, Jean Paul. 1989. *No Exit and Three Other Plays.* New York: Vintage Books.

Schwartz, Jeffrey. 1997. Cited in "For the Obsessed, the Mind Can Fix the Brain." *Newsweek,* February 26th, 60.

Seligman, Martin. 1990. *Learned Optimism: How to Change Your Mind and Your Life.* New York: Pocketbooks.

Vaughan, Peggy. 1998. *The Monogamy Myth.* New York: Newmarket Press.

Wadsworth, Barry. 1971. *Piaget's Theory of Cognitive Development.* New York: David McKay Co.

Wallerstein, Judith, and B. Blakeslee. 1989. *Second Chances: Men, Women and Children a Decade After Divorce.* New York: Ticknor and Fields.

Winicott, D. W. 1965. *The Maturational Processes and the Facilitating Environment.* New York: International Universities Press.

Wynne, L. C., I. M. Rhyckoff, J. Day, and S. I. Hirsch. 1958. "Pseudo-mutuality in the Family Relations of Schizophrenics." *Psychiatry* 21:205–220.

Some Other New Harbinger Self-Help Titles

High on Stress: A Woman's Guide to Optimizing the Stress in Her Life, $13.95
Infidelity: A Survival Guide, $13.95
Stop Walking on Eggshells, $14.95
Consumer's Guide to Psychiatric Drugs, $13.95
The Fibromyalgia Advocate: Getting the Support You Need to Cope with Fibromyalgia and Myofascial Pain, $18.95
Healing Fear: New Approaches to Overcoming Anxiety, $16.95
Working Anger: Preventing and Resolving Conflict on the Job, $12.95
Sex Smart: How Your Childhood Shaped Your Sexual Life and What to Do About It, $14.95
You Can Free Yourself From Alcohol & Drugs, $13.95
Amongst Ourselves: A Self-Help Guide to Living with Dissociative Identity Disorder, $14.95
Healthy Living with Diabetes, $13.95
Dr. Carl Robinson's Basic Baby Care, $10.95
Better Boundaries: Owning and Treasuring Your Life, $13.95
Goodbye Good Girl, $12.95
Being, Belonging, Doing, $10.95
Thoughts & Feelings, Second Edition, $18.95
Depression: How It Happens, How It's Healed, $14.95
Trust After Trauma, $13.95
The Chemotherapy & Radiation Survival Guide, Second Edition, $14.95
Heart Therapy, $13.95
Surviving Childhood Cancer, $12.95
The Headache & Neck Pain Workbook, $14.95
Perimenopause, $13.95
The Self-Forgiveness Handbook, $12.95
A Woman's Guide to Overcoming Sexual Fear and Pain, $14.95
Mind Over Malignancy, $12.95
Treating Panic Disorder and Agoraphobia, $44.95
Scarred Soul, $13.95
The Angry Heart, $14.95
Don't Take It Personally, $12.95
Becoming a Wise Parent For Your Grown Child, $12.95
Clear Your Past, Change Your Future, $13.95
Preparing for Surgery, $17.95
The Power of Two, $12.95
It's Not OK Anymore, $13.95
The Daily Relaxer, $12.95
The Body Image Workbook, $17.95
Living with ADD, $17.95
Taking the Anxiety Out of Taking Tests, $12.95
Five Weeks to Healing Stress: The Wellness Option, $17.95
Why Children Misbehave and What to Do About It, $14.95
When Anger Hurts Your Kids, $12.95
The Addiction Workbook, $17.95
The Chronic Pain Control Workbook, Second Edition, $17.95
Fibromyalgia & Chronic Myofascial Pain Syndrome, $19.95
Flying Without Fear, $13.95
Kid Cooperation: How to Stop Yelling, Nagging & Pleading and Get Kids to Cooperate, $13.95
The Stop Smoking Workbook: Your Guide to Healthy Quitting, $17.95
Conquering Carpal Tunnel Syndrome and Other Repetitive Strain Injuries, $17.95
An End to Panic: Breakthrough Techniques for Overcoming Panic Disorder, Second Edition, $18.95
Letting Go of Anger: The 10 Most Common Anger Styles and What to Do About Them, $12.95
Messages: The Communication Skills Workbook, Second Edition, $13.95
Coping With Chronic Fatigue Syndrome: Nine Things You Can Do, $13.95
The Anxiety & Phobia Workbook, Second Edition, $18.95
The Relaxation & Stress Reduction Workbook, Fourth Edition, $17.95
Living Without Depression & Manic Depression: A Workbook for Maintaining Mood Stability, $17.95
Coping With Schizophrenia: A Guide For Families, $15.95
Visualization for Change, Second Edition, $15.95
Postpartum Survival Guide, $13.95
Angry All the Time: An Emergency Guide to Anger Control, $12.95
Couple Skills: Making Your Relationship Work, $13.95
Self-Esteem, Second Edition, $13.95
I Can't Get Over It, A Handbook for Trauma Survivors, Second Edition, $16.95
Dying of Embarrassment: Help for Social Anxiety and Social Phobia, $13.95
The Depression Workbook: Living With Depression and Manic Depression, $17.95
Men & Grief: A Guide for Men Surviving the Death of a Loved One, $14.95
When Once Is Not Enough: Help for Obsessive Compulsives, $13.95
Beyond Grief: A Guide for Recovering from the Death of a Loved One, $13.95
Hypnosis for Change: A Manual of Proven Techniques, Third Edition, $15.95
When Anger Hurts, $13.95

Call toll free, **1-800-748-6273**, to order. Have your Visa or Mastercard number ready. Or send a check for the titles you want to New Harbinger Publications, Inc., 5674 Shattuck Ave., Oakland, CA 94609. Include $3.80 for the first book and 75¢ for each additional book, to cover shipping and handling. (California residents please include appropriate sales tax.) Allow two to five weeks for delivery.

Prices subject to change without notice.